Flyfishing

About the cover:
This newcomer to the world of fly-fishing caught
and released this colorful, wild, cutthroat trout
back into its native stream within seconds after
the picture was taken.

Flyfishing

First Cast to First Fish!

Joseph F. Petralia

SIERRA OUTDOOR PRODUCTS CO.®

P.O. Box 2497 • San Francisco • Ca 94126-2497

Design by Jill Applegate
Desktop Publishing by The Creative Type
Illustrations by Chickering Nelson III
Editorial Assistance by Nancy Nelson-Petralia;
                    John M. Comer

*Acknowledgment and many thanks to the following
for use of their art and / or illustrations:*
   3M Company/Scientific Anglers
   Caddis Manufacturing, Inc.
   Cortland Line Co.
   The Creek & Wood River Company
   Fenwick
   Martin Reel Co.
   O. Mustad & Son. [U.S.A.] Inc.
   Renzetti, Inc. (Fly-tying Equipment)
   Stream Designs, Inc.
   Tycoon Fin-Nor Corp.
   The Selective Angler

Published By:
Sierra Outdoor Products Company®
P.O. Box 2497
San Francisco, CA 94126

Printed in the United States of America, 1991
10 9 8 7 6 5 4 3 2 1

Library of Congress Catalog-In-Publication Data

Petralia, J. F. (Joseph F.)
   Flyfishing : first cast to first fish / Joseph F. Petralia. —

   p. cm.
   Includes bibliographical references and index.
   ISBN 0-9605890-7-4

   1. Fly fishing—Handbooks, manuals, etc.   I. Title.
SH456
799.12   90-92357

"All rivers run into the sea; yet the sea is not full; unto the place whence rivers come, thither they return again."

— ECCLESIASTES 1:7

Table of Contents

Preface

59°N 160°W—The Togiak Wilderness

...The roar of the Beaver's radial engine increased in intensity and water splashed up around the pontoons as we picked up speed and headed into the wind, taxiing across the lake's broken surface. The engine vibrated noisily and labored under the load of equipment as the pilot pushed the throttle forward to get the vintage float plane "on step," before banking slightly to break the water's grip on its pontoons. Then, suddenly we were airborne. I stared out the window in silence as we lifted off and tried to settle in for the two-hour flight that lie ahead.

This was the culmination of months of planning to bring together six friends, from as many cities, on a fly-fishing trip to the motherlode of big, strong, wild fish. Two of us had elected to fly in supplies in advance of the rest of the party to set up our base camp. We were flying at only four hundred feet of altitude and were scattering moose and bear at various points across the tundra. Off the left wing I spotted a grizzly bear loping through a slough playfully chasing a flock of sandhill crane and wondered if our group might be the object of his derision before this trip was finished.

The weather coming off the Bering Sea continued to deteriorate as we headed west and rain began pelting the windshield. The pilot continually monitored the plane's Loran unit as we picked our way through one pass to the next to our eventual drop-off point at the river's headwaters. I looked back and mentally inventoried the contents of the assorted back-packs and duffel bags that crowded the DeHavilands' cargo area. A hundred miles of river lay ahead to float and fish, but

I was satisfied that we had enough rods, reels and assorted camping and survival gear on board to handle almost any situation that came up.

Watching the tundra and wildlife pass beneath, the weather that encircled us, the rugged peaks and desolate terrain that lay ahead, one couldn't help but be over-whelmed by the grandeur and magnificence of this beautiful, green Alaskan landscape.

That trip and the many that followed was an adventure of a lifetime...and they were directly *inspired* by a love of fly-fishing and the great outdoors. ◆

*P*eople who know how much I enjoy fly-fishing in-evitably ask when it was that I started to fish. Old family snapshots that I've come across over the years, all point to starting with my father when I was barely able to hold a rod in my small hands. The addiction to fly-fishing didn't fully take hold, however, until years later when a friend, who had fly-fished for years, rekindled my interest.

Like many an Easterner before, the tales and lure of the West beckoned me to discover her past, firsthand. This led me to explore from the battlefield at the Little Big Horn to British Columbia and eventually to California's mother-lode—and, it was the latter that held me in its grip for some time.

After several summers of pursuing the elusive gold of the Sierras, I had escalated from using a simple gold pan to working an underwater gold dredge on one of my min-ing claims on the North Fork of the Yuba River.

One summer weekend I brought a friend up to the mountains to camp and look for a little "color." At the end of the day he introduced me to his streamside advocation. Don's skill as a fly fisherman, the simplicity of gear, coupled with the grace and enjoyment with which he'd catch fish, contrasted sharply with my "hobby" of gold mining, which had escalated to backbreaking, tedious, sometimes dangerous *work*.

I taught my friend how to successfully pan for gold and he showed me the rudiments of fly-fishing. We never traded hobbies, per se, but better still he took on the best of the *recreational* aspects of prospecting while maintaining his love of fly-fishing. I simply lost all interest in gold mining to pursue the many trout that I had seen while dredging from my underwater vantage point. Many years later we are still good friends, enjoying our mutual interests, often on the same stretch of water!

Using fly-fishing, perhaps as an excuse, I have ventured and adventured into places I would never have otherwise explored. Wilderness float trips in Alaska, hiking into hidden mountain lakes of the northwest's forests, to challenging the hellishly strong saltwater fish off the Baja, all I can thank to this hobby. There has been a few times when nothing seemed to work consistently and those magical times when nothing could go wrong—and I've thoroughly enjoyed them all! Fly-fishing can be the means to an end as well as the end itself. The planning, anticipation and actuation all add depth and dimension to the sport. An old Asian proverb says, "The journey is the reward..." The reason may start out to be a fishing trip in the Blue Ridge Mountains, a local lake, or distant sea, but what happens is that the sum of the whole experience becomes greater than the individual parts. The "journey" will take you and your friends to areas you might not otherwise have discovered...So, enjoy it...that's what life's about!

I hope and expect that this new world that awaits you brings you as much fun, pleasure and adventure as it has for my friends and me...*and I'm sure that it will!*

Congratulations—*you've taken the first step that will open the door to an exciting new sport.*

See you on the water...

Joe Petralia

Introduction

The World of Fly-fishing

If you've ever spent any time as a novice around fly fishermen, you undoubtedly may have been overwhelmed by a confusing amount of terminology and equipment. True, there is, as in any sport or hobby, a unique jargon, but it is not any more difficult to learn or understand than, say, a basic introduction to football or golf. The type of equipment used and the nomenclature are in some cases unique to this sport, for it is a specialized style of fishing, but it is not a difficult language to understand when broken down into the components that comprise the whole.

Fly-fishing is a method of fishing, a style, that uses equipment specifically designed for the sport. It employs a unique method of casting, a more thorough study of the fish's habits and habitat, and for me and many others, I believe, a more satisfying overall experience than dropping a chunk of bait into a pond and waiting for some action. Fly-fishing is a *pro-active* sport.

The beginnings of fishing with a fly are assumed to have begun a few thousand years ago in the cradle of civilization in Egypt, though little is known of how advanced this form of fishing was, other than what can be gleaned from early writings and drawings. The assumption is that the ancients in their pursuit of food, if not enjoyment, at some point observed fish taking insects and baitfish. In their attempt to duplicate the natural food source, and to secure these miniature creatures to their crude, handmade wood, bone and shell hooks, they soon became frustrated and came to realize that an "artificial" had to be fashioned, if it was to be able to stay on the hook long enough to do any good. Their success, or lack of same, is lost in early history.

It was not until several thousand years later, in writings that have survived to this day, that Europeans again considered the possibility of using a "lure" in the form of thread, wool, fur and feathers, arranged on a hook to imitate a natural insect, that the sport was reborn and given the foundation that initiated modern fly-fishing technique.

Much was implied in these early writings and methodology and for many years it intimidated and minimized the number of fishermen that would partake in this most enjoyable form of fishing. The idea that learning to fish with a fly rod is difficult is a myth that was perpetuated by countless anglers who have not given the sport a chance. This was either because it was thought to be an old-fashioned method (they preferred to use the latest innovations in spinning gear), they never had the information available that would logically explain it to them, or they unsuccessfully attempted to learn with inadequate equipment. So it is that the elitist aura, to some degree, still surrounds the world of fly-fishing.

Let's dispense with some of this "mystique" right from the beginning. While fly-fishing may be somewhat more difficult than passively "drowning a worm" in the local pond, it can be learned and successfully enjoyed by almost anyone who can ride a bicycle, play a racket sport, or use a computer. Fly-fishing does take some degree of coordination and motor skills and it will also take some practice to learn to cast effectively, but what other sport or game doesn't—from learning to play golf, to learning to ski. We're *all* naturally uncomfortable in the early stages of learning something new. This is because it is unfamiliar, and we may need to use a different combination of movements or muscles, but I can assure you, the process is not that difficult, the rewards are great, and *you can do it!*

Some fly-fish as much for the pleasure of casting as for the capture of fish. The fishing is the means to an end for some, while the serenity and relaxation of fly casting on a remote stream or lake can be the end in itself. The essence of fly-fishing will become apparent as your skills improve and its "mysteries" are dispelled.

But, why fish with a fly? For a number of reasons: If you already like to fish, then you probably know that fly-fishing can be an effective way of catching fish when other methods fail. What you may or may not be aware of is that you can successfully fish for just about any species of fish that swims, from the warm water bass and panfish varieties, all species of the trout family, the anadromous steelhead and salmon, to the almost infinite variety of saltwater fish that roam the world's oceans. Be it the delicate "handpainted" Golden Trout of the western mountains' alpine lakes to tarpon and shark too heavy to lift—all are being caught by today's fly-fisher.

Additionally, in today's world of increasing pressures on our fisheries, conservation is a legitimate concern. Fish caught on a fly can be released unharmed much more easily than with either lures or bait. The challenge of presenting an *artificial*, tied to represent a natural, also offers a greater degree of satisfaction and is a more sporting way of fishing. Fly-fishing means fishing with a virtually weightless fly, without the encumbrance of a heavy lure or sinker, so the fight is directly between you and the fish. The excitement, visual reward and enormous satisfaction of actually seeing a fish move to and strike your fly is an experience that will need no further explanation. The lightweight tackle, the beauty and esthetics of the equipment, and the delicacy of a handmade fly all add to the grace, timelessness and pleasure of this fascinating sport. *Fly-fishing is fun!*

Fly-fishing is also a challenge. Although it is not difficult to get started, it takes a certain level of patience and persistence to explore its full potential. That is what makes it so interesting and rewarding and what will keep you captivated. It exercises the body and the mind. The sport is also rich enough in dimension to reap by-products in the related hobbies of tackle collecting, fly-tying and participation and sharing of ideas in prestigious international organizations such as Trout Unlimited and The Federation of Fly Fishers who have played host to world leaders and presidents alike. *Fly-fishing offers a lifetime of fun and entertainment.*

◆ ◆ ◆

*T*his book is meant to be a tool, a working manual to take with you as you practice casting and as a reference source to be taken on your first trip—or on many trips thereafter. It will provide you not only with basic "how-to" information but also as a structure and reference as you seek out more information on individual, more specialized areas of fly-fishing. It should and will develop a thought process to analyze and solve various situations involving the selection of equipment, the proper fly, casting technique, locating fish and problem-solving as you develop experience and competence.

You can read this book slowly or read it fast, but *go through the WHOLE book one time just to get an overview of what fly-fishing is all about.* Don't let the sections on rod and line weights and leader X-sizes or the information on flies or equipment overwhelm you. *It is not difficult to get started.* The information is here simply for your use as you grow into the sport. Read the book first for a basic understanding…then narrow down and reread each section again for a more thorough understanding of the specifics that you need to get started. Take the book with you when you begin to practice casting and when you go on a fishing trip as a handy guide in which to refer. It *will* get you your first fish caught on a fly!

There is nothing as serene as watching an accomplished

fly caster fluidly weave the magic of his fly line through the warm summer evening air. The long, graceful loops reach out across the pristine waters of a mountain stream to its waiting trout. *There are few things as pleasurable as being that angler!*

This book will also, I hope, inspire you to seek out new areas to explore, which this sport will undoubtedly draw you, and help act in harmony and protect the environment within which we all live and play. If this book helps in this regard and aids in perpetuating the sport and the fisheries ...then I have succeeded.

I hope you'll find what follows to be a clear, definitive outline—a guide, if you will—through the maze of fly-fishing terminology relating to line weights, rod weights, line tapers, flies, dressings, etc., etc., etc.

The waters are calling...fish are waiting...and time's a wasting...*So...**let's get to it!***

THE BASICS OF FLY-FISHING

Getting Started — The Basics

1

W**hat is fly-fishing** and how does it differ from other methods of fishing?

If you've fished at all, you would have used a rod, reel, line and some form of bait or lure to entice the fish. The equipment would vary depending on the locale and type of fishing that you were doing, but you would have likely used a level-wind, bait casting or spinning reel. To the end of the thin, monofilament line would be attached the "terminal tackle" consisting of the lure, sinker, bait, bobber or other combination of *weighted* attractant.

If you were boat or bank fishing, you would simply engage the reel to its free-spool mode and let your lure or bait drop into the water, the weight of the terminal tackle drawing the line from the reel. To cast, you would pick a spot on the water, pull the rod back and cast to it. The *weight* of the lure or bait exerts its mass to withdraw the line from the reel, carrying the line with it—thus, the weight of the "terminal tackle" acts as the impetus, much as the pendulum acts on the end of a piece of string. *The weight of the lure, bait, bobber, etc., overpowers the resistance of the reel's spool, the fine diameter line ("thin" when compared to a fly line) is withdrawn, and the cast completed.*

It works, and works well, being a proven way of fishing for many, many years...but this method of fishing differs significantly in the design, operation and intent of fly-fishing and its related equipment.

The Distinction

Fly-fishing takes a different approach to fool a fish than either bait or spin-fishing. When you fly-fish you cast a virtually weightless hook, tied and disguised with bits of fur and feather, onto or into water that you've predetermined holds fish. Your manipulation of the fly mimics the natural insect, bug, baitfish or other food stuff that it represents, and in doing so induces and deceives the fish into taking it for the natural.

Fly-fishing, or more accurately fly casting, differs further from spin or bait casting as follows: a fly rod, regardless of material, is designed to cast *a specific weight of fly line.* The assembled rod, reel and line *are a component system.* (NOTE: We say *fly rod*, a minor technicality, however, using the term fly pole will not ingratiate you with many diehard fly fishermen!—*LESSON #1.*) The fly line's

In fly casting, the fly line casts the fly versus the weighted lure or bait carrying the line. ▼

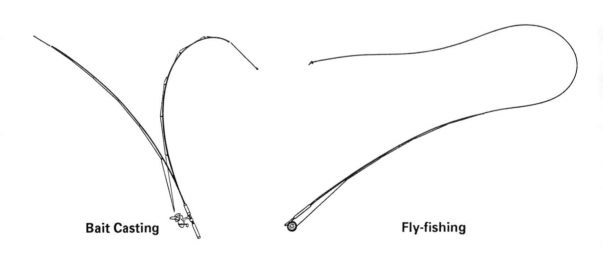

Bait Casting   **Fly-fishing**

NOTE: Technically, a rod is a manufactured, tapered stick (the so-called "blank") that is fitted with a series of guides to direct the line from the reel to the tip. The guides distinguish it from a fishing pole—the latter being a long crude stick in its natural form, without fittings, the line being tied directly to the tip of the pole. Therefore, for our purposes, there are no fly poles today but only fly rods!

thick, coated design, which we'll talk more about later on, is so engineered that as the fly rod is cast, back and then forward, the *fly line itself, by virtue of its weight,* is what is cast. The fly being relatively weightless, is carried along by the fly line. The fly reel's primary duty is to store the fly line, not revolve and unleash line, as with spin or bait casting gear.

Fly casting, therefore, distinguishes itself by *the line casting the fly (lure)* as opposed to the lure carrying out the line. This distinction will become clearer, and reinforced, as we go through the basics in the chapters that follow. The function of the rod, the line, reel, and of course, the fly... all that you'll need to get started will be explained in detail. You'll learn what it takes to cast and "present" the fly, the most likely area to find fish, and all the terms, phraseology and equipment that you'll run across as you get involved in this new sport. You should take a few minutes before getting started to review the glossary in the last chapter. Familiarize yourself with the "lingo" that fly-fishing employs and refer to it, as necessary, to further explain any term or point that needs clarification. *A whole new world is about to open up to you!*

The Nomenclature

▮ The Fly

I've heard the term *flies* for some time now—*what is a fly?* A fly is the general term used to refer to the "hook" used in fly-fishing that is dressed with feathers, fur, natural and synthetic materials, tied together with thread and a drop of glue, fabricated to imitate an insect, baitfish or other natural foodstuff that fish eat. The term "fly" is used whether or not the insect ever did have wings or flew. The fly may be a "bug," or may even be made to replicate a frog or small mammal, such as a mouse. The fly may be fished in a way to imitate

Wing
Cheek
Head
Tail
Tag
Butt
Body
Rib
Hackle (throat)

a hatching insect or a dead one, a swimming creature, a sunning frog or even a free-floating salmonoid egg. *All* are referred to as "flies."

Flies break down into several basic types: there are *dry-flies, wet-flies, nymphs, streamers, bucktails, terrestrials* and *bugs.*

Dry-flies are what their name implies, in that they are meant to remain relatively dry and to float on the water's surface. Dry-flies are tied with materials that are stiff enough to suspend the fly perkily atop the water's surface tension, buoyant enough to float, and light enough to do both. Hook size and the thickness of the hook's wire all add to this end.

A dry-fly may imitate an insect that has either been blown unwillingly into the water, has landed on the water to lay eggs, or fallen into the water, dead. Flies are tied to either closely resemble the natural or more loosely act as an attractant, edible to the fish. The dry-fly almost always is formed to as closely duplicate the natural as possible, from its size, relative to the natural insect, to the slant and color of its wings. This is because the majority of the time fish are eating below the surface, as opportunities present themselves. When they do feed on a surface fly, they usually have the luxury of being able to take a few seconds to follow it and to examine and compare it to other insects taken in the past. Their eyesight and the underwater perspective for doing so are ideal, thus the need to present an imitation that looks and acts like what a fish expects, or you will not interest it. But, when you do get that strike—*expect to begin the dry-fly addiction!*

Wet-flies, conversely, are meant to probe below the water's surface and imitate drowned, drifting or hatching insects. Toward that end, they're either tied more sparsely than a dry-fly, with materials that quickly absorb water and/or tied onto a heavier hook wire. In years gone by, it was fairly standard practice to tie on two, three, and as many as five wet-flies onto one's leader. The idea was that

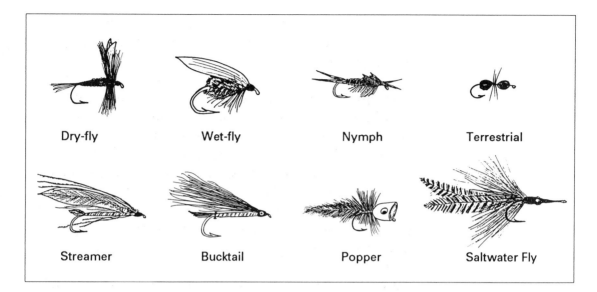

Dry-fly	Wet-fly	Nymph	Terrestrial
Streamer	Bucktail	Popper	Saltwater Fly

Flies break down into several basic types. ▲

as each was swept along beneath the water, one of the patterns selected would be more apt to tempt a fish than the next, thereby assuring oneself of good luck.

It also was expected that if several flies were fished at once, each would sink at varying depths, and being flushed along as they were, one or more would cross the territory of a fish and surely invite a successful strike.

Somewhat akin to the wet-fly is the **nymph**. Fished "wet" the nymph is a more specialized type of wet-fly. Its purpose is to imitate an immature form of insect life that is in a transitional period between its larval/nymphal stage and a mature adult. Its form is more closely aligned to the natural and is generally fished with a much shorter line in a very specific manner. Nymphing is probably the most difficult technique to successfully master, but it also can be the most effective method.

Streamers and **bucktails** are the next category. These are also considered "wet" flies since they also do their work below the water. Streamers and bucktails are tied to imitate baitfish or forage fish and, as such, act in much the same manner as lures do. Their erratic behavior, dictated by their placement and activation by the angler, has been known to take many large fish. Streamers/bucktails can be a very reliable means to save an otherwise fishless day.

Terrestrials, or land-dwelling creatures, fit into the next category. They can include everything from crickets, grasshoppers, caterpillars, small rodents, beetles, ants, and the like, that find themselves unwillingly set upon the water. These are generally considered to be "drys."

Next come the *bugs*, or so-called popping bugs, sometimes generally referred to as bass bugs. These are made either with deer-hair that is tied, expanded, and trimmed with a scissor to provide a cup in the front so they pop when retrieved, or made from soft, lightweight balsa wood, cork or synthetic material. These may also be outfitted with thin rubber legs or bead eyes to give them more life-like action.

Saltwater "flies" generally fall into the "wet" category and are usually of a larger size, made of more durable material to resist the corrosive action of the salt. They will imitate everything from forage fish to shrimp and small crabs, in effect, whatever looks edible to the fish in their natural environment. The same prerequisite as in each of the categories listed above.

The successful presentation of the right type of fly, in the right place, fished in the appropriate manner, coupled with your being able to visually and sometimes audibly hear the strike (which can be as gentle as a "slurp" to a vicious slash) definitely will get your motor going, even, or sometimes especially, if you *miss that strike!* You'll want more—and more. So it goes that there are fly-fishers that adjust their method to suit conditions and those who love to see the "take" so much that they can rarely break themselves away from using anything other than dry-flies, even when it defies better judgment. You decide for yourself. Whatever gives you the most enjoyment is the right course for you. *Fly-fishing is not simply a game of how many fish you can catch but how much fun it is to do it!*

▪ Hooks

Hooks, onto which flies are tied, come in a variety of styles and sizes for various applications and fly patterns, ranging from the largest 5/0 size to the tiny #28. The hook itself consists of several parts: the eye, shank, its bend, point and the "gap," that is, the space between the shank and the point. Depending on the type and pattern of the fly and what it is to imitate, the tier will select from a number of variables offered by the hook manufacturer. This will take into account whether the hook has an up or down-turned eye, the thickness, material and/or finish of the wire itself, length of the shank (standard length or otherwise), the hook "style" and whether the point is barbed or "barbless." Once selected, tiny insects to large baitfish and terrestrials will be constructed upon the hook by either workers contracted by a manufacturer, a custom fly-tier or the individual fly-fishing enthusiast.

The accompanying chart will give you a frame of reference, although different patterns may make one fly appear slightly larger or smaller on the same "size" hook. You can use the hook size as a guide as you select a fly and pattern that most closely matches the natural.

Hook Sizes (drawn to scale)

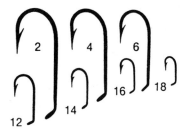

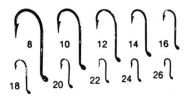

Down-turned Eye *(standard wire)*   Up-turned Eye *(extra fine wire)*

Courtesy of O. Mustad & Son [USA] Inc.

▮ The Fly Rod

Fly rods are manufactured from bamboo, fiberglass, graphite, and combinations of synthetic materials, by a host of manufacturers. The fly rod's primary function is to cast the fly line and deliver the fly. Toward that end, various manufacturers have their own design formula regarding materials, tapers, stiffness, etc., that determine the particular characteristics of a given brand or model.

Some rods will have a slower or softer action, others a stiffer, quicker action. One may be softer in the forward section, another having a more progressive response throughout its length, from tip through the butt section. All, however, are designed to cast a given weight line. Some rods may be more forgiving than others and will take a line weight higher or lower than that recommended by the manufacturer, but *the rod maker engineered each model to optimally cast a specific line weight.* The correct rod and matching line are what is called a "balanced out-fit," and it is critical in fly casting. The rod, when cast, will flex and "load" as the rod material resists the pressure of the correct line. The stored energy will power the line forward (or back) based on a combination of the power of the cast, the rod's design, and the style of line.

The rod consists of a ***reel-seat*** and sliding or screw-type threads to hold the reel, a ***handle***, usually of cork, the rod "blank" itself, and a series of ***guides*** mounted along its length. The rod may have two-pieces or, if it's a packable "travel" rod, three or more sections, each section joined by a *ferrule*. Often there is also a small **hook keeper** ring or wire hoop mounted just above the handle. The first guide, positioned 20–22 inches above the handle, is the so-called **stripping guide** and has a larger diameter opening to accommodate the line being fed from the reel. The rest of the **snake guides** are spaced to distribute the pressure and weight of a hooked fish evenly along the length of the rod. Better manufacturers usually have at least one guide for each foot of a rod's length, progressively, not evenly, spaced.

The specifications of each rod are usually found imprinted on the rod blank along the butt section, above the handle (i.e., Fenwick 9' for 6 weight line), possibly with a model name. Remember, fly rod and line weight go hand-in-hand.

About thirty years ago the American Fishing Tackle Manufacturers Association (AFTMA) standardized the coding of fly lines. Fly lines are now referred to by a number or weight designation. Line weights start with No. 1, the lightest, finest diameter, through No. 16, the heaviest. The rods that accommodate these line weights, at either end of the spectrum, are speciality rods. The No. 1–2–3–4 lines, and the rods to which they're mated, cast the lightest flies and make the most delicate "presentation,"

Fly rod specifications are indicated on the butt section. ▲

which may be necessary in certain situations. The high-end weights cast larger, more wind-resistant flies, such as those used in bass fishing and/or saltwater conditions where presentation is less critical, but where either distance, wind, weight or the air-resistance of the fly need to be overcome.

A fly rod and line are therefore selected based on intended use. A shorter rod of 7–8' may be easier to handle in smaller creeks and bushy areas, while an 8½' or 9½' rod will facilitate casting onto the larger waters of the west and maintain better line control. It will also help make higher back casts, keeping line and fly clear of high banks and brush.

The selection of your first fly rod can be an intimidating proposition, but it needn't be. Although there have never been more fly rods to choose from, the competition between a wealth of manufacturers, new space-age rod materials, diversity of lengths, "actions" and tapers offer fly rods for every budget and type of fishing. This may initially seem to make the selection process more difficult, but in fact, actually helps you to focus on and select a rod for the type of fishing that you like to do the most. So, let's narrow down the field.

The first question you need to ask yourself, or will be asked of you by someone helping you make a rod selection, is the kind of fishing that you expect to be doing. This will narrow down the rod's line weight and, to some degree, the length. The various names with which rods are tagged hint to their intended purpose. "Bass rod," "Spring Creek" and "Tarpon Special" broadly define the parameters they are intended to fish—the rod suiting the fishing condition. The line weight that the rod casts is a function of its mass. The lighter weights, while requiring a greater degree of timing, disturb the water the least and make a more delicate presentation in still water conditions or to skittish fish. The lighter weight and small silhouette of a No. 2 or 3 weight lines make them ideal for casting small flies (#16–#28) with

Fly Line Weight *vs.* Intended Fishing

FLY LINE WEIGHT	PRESENTATION	FLY SIZE	SPECIES
No. 1	Ultra light	18–28	Trout/Panfish *(Crappie, Blue Gill, Sun Fish, etc.)*
No. 2	Ultra light	18–28	Trout/Panfish
No. 3	Light	16–24	Trout/Smallmouth bass
No. 4	Light	16–24	Trout/Smallmouth bass
No. 5	Light/Medium	14–22	Trout/Smallmouth bass
No. 6	Medium	14–22	Trout/Summer steelhead
No. 7	Medium	12–20	Trout/Largemouth bass
No. 8	Medium/Heavy	12–16	Pike/Shad
No. 9	Medium/Heavy	10–12	Bonito/Striped bass Winter-run steelhead
No. 10	Medium/Heavy	12–2	Bone fish/Snook
No. 11	Heavy	12–2/0	Tarpon/Tuna
No. 12–16	Very heavy	2–2/0+	Billfish

This chart is a general guide only. Note, as rod/fly line weights increase, larger, more wind-resistant and/or weighted flies can be used for larger, more powerful fish.

the lightest (5X–8X) tippets on beaver ponds and spring creeks, and the lighter rod, to which they're matched, will make a small fish feel like a lion. Windy conditions or large flies, however, will make these lighter lines difficult to cast. Although there are no hard-and-fast rules between where one line weight leaves off and another begins, 4 and 5 weight lines obviously represent a step up in mass and become easier to cast in breezy conditions with some sacrifice in delicacy. They can also efficiently handle somewhat larger dry-flies (#14–24) and small to medium size streamers (#4 and smaller).

As you approach the mid-point of line weights (No. 5–6–7), you're looking at a good, all-around weight for casting larger, more wind-resistant flies, for catching everything from panfish to trout and bass, with dry flies, wets, nymphs and streamers. The No. 7–8–9 lines switch the balance over to power versus delicacy and will cast further, cast better in windy conditions and handle larger, bushier flies, as well as weighted nymphs and poppers. They are used in more open waters where distance casting is important and are favored by both bass, salmon and steelhead fishermen, as well as light-tackle, saltwater enthusiasts.

As with the lightest lines, the high-end of the scale at No. 10–11–12, right on up to No. 16 weight, are "speciality" lines. They will cast the heaviest, most wind-resistant flies and are generally favored by salmon and saltwater fishermen who rely on larger flies to attract their quarry. Although these lines and their matching rods can be fatiguing to cast for long periods, they do, in the hands of an experienced fly caster, throw a line a long way without a lot of false casting.

Unless you live near a particular stretch of water or plan to do a lot of speciality fishing, your first rod and training tool would best be one selected from the mid-range. This will cover your needs for most of the fish you're likely to encounter and will become the backbone of your collection.

Rod lengths will range from as short as 6½–7' to 16' double handed models favored in the open Fjords of northern Europe. The most versatile and most popular lengths, by far, are in the 8–9' range. Shorter models require a greater degree of finesse and timing to cast well, and the longest lengths, when matched to the heavier lines to which they're tailored, are not nearly as much fun to cast or on which to learn.

Okay, so you know pretty much the type of fishing you expect to be doing and, since you'll want it to suit a range of fish types and conditions, you'll probably want to start with a fly rod and line in the mid-range. A 5 or 6 weight fly line matched to an 8½–9' rod is therefore a good choice. So now what?

Here's where the fun begins. Somewhere close to where you live there is certainly a sporting goods store that has a selection of fly-fishing equipment. Better yet, there may be a fly-fishing shop. There are also a dozen plus excellent mail-order houses that specialize in fly-fishing equipment to fit every budget (see RESOURCES CHAPTER). The obvious advantage of a fly shop is the selection of rods that you'll be able to review and try out as well as the expert guidance of the personnel.

Look at the various manufacturers' rods in the length and weight that you've predetermined. Have the store clerk load the rod with reel and line and, if possible, make a few practice casts. Your rod should feel like an extension of your arm as it will communicate to you the action of the line and telegraph the strike of a fish. Different materials, tapers and models will "feel" different—some subtle, some not so subtle. Fiberglass rods are generally lower in price than graphite, but graphite and graphite-rich composition rods will enable you to cast more easily, cast further, and enhance your learning speed. Ideally, one rod will feel more responsive than the other and will not take a lot of concentration to cast or excessive time to get used to. What "feels" best for you, might not necessarily be best for your friend. "Test-driving," so to speak, several models will more than likely separate one or two rods from the rest of the lot.

There are also a number of rod–reel–fly line "beginners' packages" available, matching all the components into one unit. In the better name brands, I'm sure they're fine but I've had the opportunity to try a couple of the economy packages that were priced under $100 and feel that too much was sacrificed for the sake of price. Avoid the so-called "combination" rods, those purported to serve with either a spinning reel or, by quickly reversing the handle, a fly reel. They may work okay with the former, but are generally too soft to ever be satisfactory as a fly rod. Unless your budget is very tight, I'd suggest that you buy and match individual, separate, components to suit your personal taste and pocketbook. *Shopping for your equipment is part of the fun!*

■ The Fly Line

In fishing, other than fly-fishing, the fishing line is a "thin" monofilament or braided dacron line. Its function is simply to remain attached to the lure/bait and hook. In fly-fishing, as we now know, the fly line casts the fly, but its design goes beyond merely just its weight. Modern fly lines have several variables built into them and are therefore very versatile: by altering a fly line's core material (flexibility), the amount (weight), distribution (taper) and density (function) of its plastic coating, a manufacturer can give a line a number of special performance features to enhance the natural presentation of your fly.

A fly line is approximately thirty *yards* long and its weight (in grams) is based on its first 30 *feet* of line. Fly lines are available in a variety of *colors*, *tapers*, and *functions* for each line number or *"weight."* Each of these specifications is clearly marked on the fly line box at the point of purchase, as will be outlined in a minute.

Fly lines are manufactured in several different silhouettes or **tapers**. Given each silhouette, the thickness of the plastic coating is varied to put either more or less weight in the forward section of the line, thus giving the line the ability to either make longer casts more easily or, conversely, formed with less weight in the forward end and a finer longer taper, to make a more delicate *presentation* or landing of the fly, as may sometimes be necessary.

TIP 1.0'
STANDARD WEIGHT FORWARD FLOATING LINE (#8 LINE WEIGHT)
RUNNING LINE 42.5'
FRONT TAPER 6.0'
BELLY 30.5'
CORE   COATING
REAR TAPER 3.5'

The next consideration is the *function* of the line once it lands on the water. Fly lines are made to float, or to sink at varying rates, or a combination of both abilities incorporated into one line. Dry-flies obviously require a floating line, while wet-flies including nymphs, streamers and the like, can be fished with either a floating, sinking or sink-tip line. Lake versus stream fishing, for example, may require a full sinking line of rather rapid descending properties.

Fly line cross-section

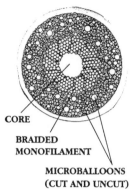

CORE

BRAIDED
MONOFILAMENT

MICROBALLOONS
(CUT AND UNCUT)

Then there is *color*. Less important than either weight, taper or function, color does play a role. Given bright water conditions, a highly visible line will make it easier for the fly-fisher to follow his line, both for proper loop control in casting as well as in detecting strikes when fishing wet(s). High visibility lines rarely spook fish, given the brighter background that they're cast against, while dull, non-glare colors/finishes can aid the angler in the bright, glaring conditions of the "flats" or in the saltwater tropics when fishing for bonefish and the like.

The weight, taper, function and color define the fly line's character.

Weight, by necessity, is dictated by the rod, the latter which was selected by the type of fishing you'll be doing most often, as outlined earlier. As we know, it is critically important to start with a balanced rod and fly line. To do otherwise would only unnecessarily handicap your ability to learn to cast and frustrate your entry into fly-fishing. So the assumption is that your six-weight rod, for instance, will be correctly "loaded" with a six-weight line.

Line taper is a somewhat more personal choice. Modern fly line manufacturing techniques enable the line manufacturer to impart varying degrees of taper into the overall silhouette of the fly line, as illustrated. So your choice, again, should be selected on the basis of your intended use. I'd suggest starting out with a double taper line as your first line for several reasons that will soon become apparent.

Fly Line Configurations

Level

Double Taper

Rocket Taper

Bass Taper

Saltwater Taper

Shooting Taper

Weight Forward Fly Lines

(Courtesy of the Cortland Line Co.)

∎ Line Types

Level (L) lines are generally the most economical to manufacture and therefore the cheapest to purchase. They are uniform in diameter from one end to the next and have major limitations in their ability to be easily cast, cast well or make a decent, delicate presentation. Unless there is a severe need to restrict your budget, there is false economy in beginning with a level line.

Double taper (DT) lines are, as their name implies, tapered equally at either end of the fly line. These are probably the most popular as a floating line for a number of reasons. Since the line has a level center section that tapers to a fine point at either end, it can make a gentle delivery and is less likely to spook fish. Double tapers are also easier to roll-cast in tight situations. As an added bonus, should the forward section become prematurely worn out, as it is more apt to do in a beginner's situation, the worn end of the line can simply be rewound onto the rear end of the reel, thus putting the other "new" end forward and adding true meaning to the term *double* taper.

Weight forward (WF) lines have a greater degree of

relative weight incorporated into the plastic coating on the forward portion of the line, tapering back to a fine diameter "running" line, enabling them to be cast further and with less line out from the rod tip. They do sacrifice a bit of delicacy since there is a shorter length of fine taper between the weight forward section and the tippet/fly. A *bass bug taper* or *saltwater taper* is even more exaggerated in its "weight forward" configuration, but again, the weight helps in casting large, wind-resistant flies that generally aren't intended to land very softly anyway.

Dual density combination lines are also available for those times when neither a floating nor sinking line is the best choice. **Floating/sinking** (F/S) or "sink-tip" lines combine a high density sinking "head" of 10 or 15 feet, coupled with a floating line, mated as one. This forward section of the fly line usually has a different or darker color to distinguish it from the floating portion or, in some cases, a bright visible section at the junction to aid in strike detection. The F/S should not be a first choice but is a specialty line that gives you the ability to more easily mend (reposition) or lift a sunken line, since only a portion of the line is submerged. A floating/sinking line is handy for probing the subsurface when it becomes impractical to continue to add weight to a tippet or fly in order to reach the fish's feeding level.

Sinking (S), or more accurately *full sinking* lines, will sink/submerge throughout their entire length. These are available in various rates of sinking speeds and are used primarily in still water situations where it is necessary to go down deep. They are more difficult to lift from the water than either a floating or sink-tip line, but do sink deeply and are usually the line of choice for fishing lakes.

For the sake of reference there is one other type of fly line in the speciality area that you'll run across and may eventually want to add to your inventory as your abilities and your appetite for fishing under varying conditions increases. These are not meant for a gentle presentation, but for distance casting on large and/or swift waters. This is the ***shooting taper*** (ST) or shooting head. Relatively short in length, usually about 30 feet or a third the length of a "regular" fly line, shooting tapers correspond to the weight-forward, front-end portion of a fly line. Instead of being bonded, as one, directly to a floating line, the "head" is attached to a running or shooting line by means of a loop (for quick change). Level line, if available in a fine enough diameter, can be successfully used as "running" line, coupled with a shooting taper at its forward end. The high density, weight-forward design of the shooting head, combined with the minimal resistance of a fine shooting line, creates a long distance casting vehicle. Shooting tapers are available in a wide range of densities from moderate to ultra-fast sinking speeds.

▮ Decoding the Fly Line Box

The specifics of taper-weight, taper, function and color are easily distinguishable on the fly box itself, in the following order: taper, line weight, function.

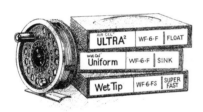

A double taper, six-weight, floating line would be encoded on the fly box as DT-6-F, while a weight forward, eight-weight, full sinking line would be read as WF-8-S, and so on. Color, while not encoded as above, is usually printed on the box or visible through the clear plastic wrapper.

Taper/Line Types:

· Level — L	· Shooting Taper — ST
· Double Taper — DT	· Floating — F
· Weight forward — WF	· Sinking — S
· Sink-tip — F/S	· Intermediate (sinking) — I

A full listing of fly lines, tapers, weights, etc., is available from either 3-M/Scientific Anglers or Cortland Line Company. They offer a dizzying array of lines to suit every purpose—and every pocketbook.

▮ Leaders

The leader is a section of monofilament between the forward end of your fly line and the fly. The leader's dual function is to continue the transmittal of energy of the fly rod and line, and, while maintaining an almost invisible connection to the fly, deliver the fly to the fish.

Leaders are broadly divided into two styles: one-piece *knotless,* and *compound* "knotted" leaders. Each has its own following and advantages.

Knotless leaders, somewhat akin to fly line, are now being offered in a variety of "tapers," stepping down from the stiffer butt section to the finer tippet in greater or lesser degrees of change. The idea is to aid in the presentation of the fly. The heavier, more air-resistant the fly, the more need to taper quickly, or risk having the tippet collapse and fail to properly transfer the energy and deliver the fly. Conversely, long, finer tapers still turn over the smaller flies while maintaining and contributing to a delicate, natural delivery—and hence, more hookups!

The knotless variety has become much more popular in recent years simply because it is less labor intensive to produce and the technology has improved along with the leader material. It is also generally available in sporting goods stores that don't carry a full fly-fishing section. Knotless leaders offer the advantage of not having knots that can hang up moss or other small debris present in some waters. Some brands, however, can be too soft in the butt section and may not always turn over a fly as effectively as a compound leader.

Compound leaders are made by joining successively thinner sections of leader material together by barrel or blood knots. These are available at fly shops or can be made by the average fisherman at home or streamside at a fraction of the cost of the store-bought variety. Compound leaders can be made in an infinite number of "formulas," graduating their taper to customize them to your rod and line. "Leader kits," consisting of spools of leader material of assorted diameters and formulas for tying same, are available at most fly shops and through catalog houses.

Braided leaders, the latest entry onto the marketplace, offer a third option. Thin strands of a monofilament material are woven into a braid, tapering towards its forward end. To the end of the "braid" a section of tippet material is tied in, the braided leader now complete. Given the engineering of the braid and its taper, the leader will stiffen under a quick, firm cast, yet relax and behave in a supple fashion, after delivery, to present the fly in a drag-free attitude. Braided leaders are relatively costly and their construction necessitates some unusual methods of attachment to both the fly line and the tippet, usually with one of the "Super Glue" type adhesives.

A good leader will be designed from a material that has high strength for its diameter, a taper designed to efficiently transfer the rod and line's energy (in order to turn over and deliver the fly), and a low drag co-efficient, thereby allowing the fly to drift naturally. A leader needs to complement and *balance* with the fly line, the fly and the fishing conditions.

The leader/tippet design is expected to transfer the energy of the unrolling fly line and deliver or *present* the fly in a realistic manner. Too light a tippet matched to too large a fly will collapse on the water around the fly. Conversely, a light fly tied to a leader that is too stout will make a heavy-handed presentation of the fly, useful in only certain specialized situations as covered elsewhere in this book. This is just one of the reasons why you need to observe your fly as it lands.

The *tippet* is the end (finest section) of either a knotless or compound leader to which you tie on the fly. The term *tippet* also refers to *tippet material* which can be *added* to an existing leader that has become nicked, frayed or shortened. Thus, the hair-thin tippet is the almost invisible connection between the fly and line, making that connection as remote to the fish as possible.

Knotless tapered leaders, compound leaders as well as tippet material are packaged by X-size, that is, by a code that designates its diameter. The scale begins at 0X for the largest, 1X for the next largest, and so on down to the cobweb fine 8X size. The X-size of the leader/tippet will be a factor in its breaking strength, but since there is only standardization as to the X-size code, manufacturers will mark their individual brand's "test" strength on its packaging.

By matching up the correct leader/tippet X-size to your fly, within the range defined in the accompanying chart, you assure yourself that the leader correctly *turns over* (unrolls the fly line, leader and fly) in the appropriate manner. The following chart should help as a guide:

Correct Balanced Relationship of Tippet to Hook Size

X-Size	Tippet Diameter (inches)	Recommended Hook Size
0X	.011	1/0–4
1X	.010	4–8
2X	.009	6–10
3X	.008	10–14
4X	.007	12–16
5X	.006	14–22
6X	.005	16–24
7X	.004	18–26
8X	.003	18–28

The X-size (diameter) of the tippet, as it relates to the fly used, is more critical than the breaking strength, particularly in dry-fly fishing where presentation is more crucial. Generally, I will use a size or two larger tippet (lower number X-size) when fishing wets/streamers, because the presentation is less critical, strikes are harder, fish are heavier, and, when fighting downstream currents, it gives me a higher confidence level.

Regardless of leader type, to properly turn over and accurately present the fly, a leader must be straightened prior to use to uncoil the loops set into it from being stored either in its packaging or on the fly reel. This is easily done by slowly drawing the leader, from butt section to tippet, through the fingers several times. The warmth created by the friction and the gradual pulling will straighten it so as to lay out your fly into its intended target zone.

A word to the wise that you may want to file for future reference: different brands of leader material aren't always compatible with other brands of tippet material. I lost three good fish in a row one morning, breaking each one off at the junction of the leader and tippet knot. Afterwards, I found out that the leader material (Brand A) was a soft, supple variety. The tippet material (Brand B), though also supple, had a harder outer coating which, when under tension, cut through and severed the leader where it was joined at the knot! Ask when you buy your leaders if the brand that you've selected is compatible with your tippet material. Also, keep in mind that leader/tippet materials lose strength and deteriorate with age, heat or in direct sunlight. So, protect and keep your supply fresh.

▌ Fly Reels

Fly reels, like fly rods and their history and collection, can be and are a hobby unto themselves. Collectors have probably been enamored with fly reels since they were first available. These simple, yet intriguing, mechanical devices each portray a bit of the maker's art and ingenuity both in function and style. I won't cloud the issue and address the extensive historical or collectible aspect of the fly reel, but stick to its function as it relates to the newcomer venturing into the sport. What concerns us is the reel as

Single Action

Multiplying

Automatic

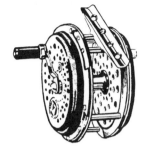

"Rim Control" single action reel
Courtesy of 3M/Scientific Anglers

Multiplying and Automatic Reels
Courtesy of The Martin Reel Company

it pertains to the system as a whole. The separate field of collection can be pursued once a frame of reference can be made to compare the many makers of the past.

The fly reel was originally designed as a convenient place to store the fly line as it was being played out either during casting or after the retrieval of a fish. As such, apart from its aesthetic appeal, it didn't have much demand placed on it. Often it is still used simply in that capacity. Yet, once one begins to hunt and take quarry larger than a half dozen inches, playing the larger fish off the reel becomes increasingly more important. Fly-fishing today means angling for all kinds of fish. This may mean very selective, wary trout using light lines and delicate tippets, or some big, hard-fighting, long-running species. Therefore, the quality, design, added features and investment in a decent reel soon become apparent.

Fly reels are generally broken into three basic categories; *single action*, *multiplying* and *automatic*.

Single action reels are just that: one turn of the handle equals one revolution of the spool. A more or less direct relationship with the fish.

Multiplying reels contain a gear mechanism within the reel that allows each turn of the handle to revolve the spool several times, three-to-one ratios being the norm. Somewhat heavier than an equivalent size single action fly reel, multipliers are used in specialized situations in order to retrieve a lot of line quickly such as in bass or saltwater fishing.

Automatic fly reels are noticeably heavier and bulkier since they incorporate a hand-wound spring device and a finger-operated lever which operates the spring-driven spool and retrieves any loose line.

My personal prejudices aside, the single action reel, for most situations, suits the majority of people best. It is lightweight, uncomplicated, efficient, has a higher line capacity and, most of all, the 1:1 ratio appeals to the sense of what the sport of fly-fishing embodies. This is by no means a hard-and-fast rule. If a fishing situation calls for quick line pick-up, a multiplying reel may be handier and a wise choice. You may, perhaps, receive an automatic reel as a gift or as a hand-me-down, or, because of a disability or simply personal preference, such a reel may best suit the individual. Each, in the act of casting line, offers little advantage over the next.

From the early days of fly-fishing, single action reels have been made out of wood, various stamped metals, cast brass, bronze, and, of late, machined aluminum, graphite and other lightweight compositions; the brass/bronze varieties and models with an anodized finish protect the reel from the damaging effects of the elements and salt-water corrosion.

Single action reels are modestly priced and can be quite serviceable for under $50, but may lack certain added features like a drag or rim control which enhance their ability to fight larger fish and extend their range of usefulness. The better makers (above $50) will generally offer several sizes in each model. The size of the reel's diameter/capacity will closely match the amount of a given weight line that will fit on the reel, with appropriate backing. You could, for instance, select a six weight fly rod, buy a number six reel (or appropriate manufacturer's model number) and know that it will accommodate both the backing line and the six weight line, and literally balance with the rod. Choose a smaller size reel and you will not be able to spool either sufficient backing and/or all of the number six fly line. Conversely, you could buy or inherit a reel size larger than necessary and be able to add additional backing to the spool knowing that the reel's larger size will weigh slightly more.

An adjustable drag, with or without an audible click, is an asset in playing and tiring a large fish "off the reel." *Rim control reels* are manufactured so they expose the spool's rim, thus making it accessible to be "palmed" by the none rod hand, for the purpose of slowing the fish's run and draining its power. *Ventilated spools*, add to the reel's ability to dry out line and prevent weakening of the backing material. In addition to the features mentioned above, the reel should have a *quick release button* to release the spool. This is a very handy feature that enables you to carry additional different function lines on a spare spool or two, without purchasing and/or carrying an entire second reel. Most or all of these features are inherent in the moderate priced reels and should be looked for when purchasing used equipment as well.

When deciding on a reel, as with a rod, select one (with sufficient capacity) to match the type of fishing that you plan to do. A small reel may be fine for trout but not hold enough backing line to last more than a few seconds when hooked up to a fresh steelhead. Compare its features as they relate to your pocketbook. A lower priced reel will work as an entry piece of equipment or for occasional use. A moderate or better priced reel, from a brand-name manufacturer, may be a wiser long-term investment. Comparison of several makers and models, with a little advice from the dealer, will lead you to the right choice. A quality reel will not only perform well for many seasons and provide versatility in usage, but also gives one pleasure because its aesthetics and smooth function. I've picked up a number of used fly reels at flea markets and pawn shops over the years, at a great savings over new. Initially I used these as primary fishing equipment and later as either extras or for use by a friend that I would introduce to the sport. There are some great bargains out there if you look, my best being an almost perfect but grimy looking Hardy reel that I picked up in a pawn shop in southeast Florida for $10.00. I guess that in saltwater country a freshwater fly reel was out of place and no one thought to take 5 minutes to clean it up and realize its full potential.

Look at the various brands available at retail and, if you plan to buy a new rod and reel, do it at the same time, along with the fly line, assuring yourself of a balanced outfit.

Putting it all together

In the preceding pages we have discussed the overall concept of fly-fishing and how it differentiates itself from bait and spin casting, as well as an overview of flies, fly rods, fly lines and leaders. These are the basic tools of the fly-fisher. We'll now put it all together into a *system*, literally tying together all the parts to complete the whole so we can begin learning to cast, the second basic element in our program to metamorphose into a fly-fisher.

At this point, you may find it helpful to jump ahead and preview the chapter on knots, as some of these will come into play in the assembly of our line and leaders. For now, simply familiarize yourself with those knots as they refer to connecting backing to fly line, fly line to leader, and the like, and save the rest for later.

Once you have purchased or borrowed the necessary components for a complete fly-fishing outfit, it will be necessary to organize your equipment and assemble it for use.

You should have sufficient backing line, fly line, reel, some leader material, a fly and, of course, fly rod. You'll also need a small scissors or nail clipper, and either some clear nail polish or fly-tiers head cement. Begin by deciding if you want to retrieve line, and turn the reel's handle, with either the left or right hand. The traditional form for right-handers is to cast with the rod in the right hand, set the hook, switch the rod to the left hand, and then crank the reel's handle with the right hand. (Left-handers would do the opposite, on all counts.) Personally, I've always preferred to cast right-handed and fight the fish with the rod remaining in my right hand, thereby remaining in control from cast, through strike, hook-up, and landing of the fish. Reeling the line with my left hand is perfectly comfortable and there seems to be a growing conversion of right-handed fly fishermen that agree. (Again, left-handers would cast left-handed and retrieve with the right.) Strong saltwater fish, however, may dictate that the stronger hand be used for retrieving line. Decide for yourself. Examine your reel and set it up, according to the manufacturer's instructions, for either right- or left-handed retrieval, as you choose.

Next, take the backing, which should be 20# woven or braided nylon or Dacron, and loop it around the reel's center arbor and tie a *backing* knot as illustrated. You can do this procedure either with just the reel in your hand or you can first attach the reel to the fly rod's reel seat, using only the rod's butt section. Some people find it easy to manipulate the reel and line while attached to the rod. If you prefer to have the reel on the rod, then first run the backing line through the butt's stripping guide, which is the guide closest to the reel seat, then to and around the reel's arbor and proceed to tie the knot.

Once the slip knot is pulled snugly around the reel's arbor, begin cranking the reel and applying the backing line. You can put a pencil through the center of the backing line's spool and have a friend release the line under

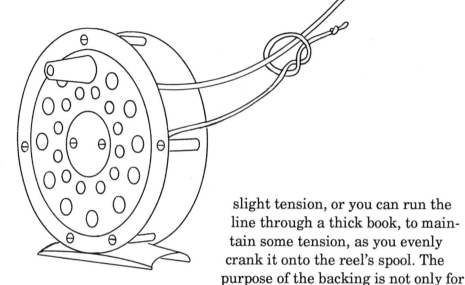

slight tension, or you can run the line through a thick book, to maintain some tension, as you evenly crank it onto the reel's spool. The purpose of the backing is not only for insurance, should a large fish take all your fly line in a run for freedom, but it also serves to fill up the spool, so the fly line lies onto it in larger, more relaxed coils. For most freshwater fly-fishing situations for trout, bass, panfish and the like, 40–60 yards of 20# backing is a comfortable margin and will fit along with the appropriate fly line on reels designed for #4 to #8 weight lines—more on some models, less on others.

Once the backing is applied, cut the line from its spool, take the *correct end* of the fly line and join the two via either a *nail* knot or an *Albright* knot. Either end of a double taper line can be joined to the backing, however, weight-forward and sink-tip lines need to be joined by their tail-end. The fly line manufacturer usually has this end marked with a small tag ("this end to reel") or it is stored in the packaging with the tail-end available first. After the knot joining the backing and fly line is tied and snugged up, carefully and neatly trim the tag ends. Clear nail polish, Pliobond, fly-tiers' head cement or other flexible coating optionally can be applied to the knot to make the joint smoother, thereby facilitating its passage through the fly rod's guides.

The fly line can now be wound onto the reel. If, however, too much backing was put on and the fly line does not fit with sufficient clearance to allow for free, unencumbered revolution of the spool, then the fly line will have to be removed, the knot cut, and some of the backing removed. After completion of the backing/fly line, select a leader and attach it to the end of the fly line by using either a *nail* knot or an *Albright* knot. The reel and line/leader now complete, you're ready to complete the assembly of rod and reel.

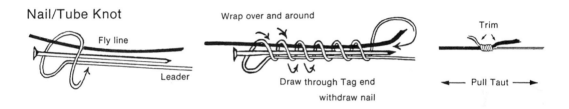

Nail/Tube Knot
Fly line
Leader
Wrap over and around
Draw through Tag end
withdraw nail
Trim
Pull Taut

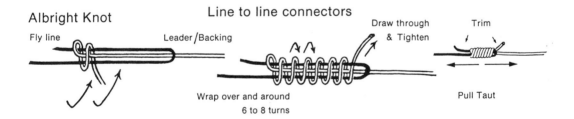

Albright Knot
Fly line
Line to line connectors
Leader/Backing
Draw through & Tighten
Trim
Wrap over and around
6 to 8 turns
Pull Taut

You'll want to put the rod together *outside*, at the site of your casting area. Rods assembled indoors or transported assembled, sustain a high incidence of damage and breakage. The rod is put together beginning with the butt section, then the second and/or third section is added. You should line up the guides *prior* to pushing the male and female sections of the ferrules together. This minimizes excessive wear at these points. Push the sections together

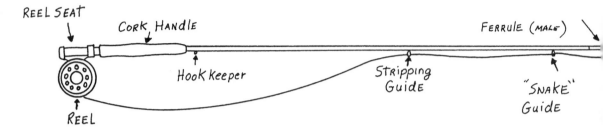

gently, do not force them or you'll have difficulty in taking them apart later. Sight down the rod to assure the guides are in alignment, set the reel's foot on the reel seat, slip the forward portion of the foot under the hooded portion of the reel seat, and turn the locking screw to secure the reel. Again, don't force anything, over-tighten or use any tools to tighten the locking nut.

Next, strip off eight or ten feet of line/leader from the reel. *Double over* the leader and begin passing it through each of the guides until you have passed it through the topmost guide (the tiptop). Doubling the line makes it easier to hang onto, gives you better visibility to thread each guide, and helps keep the line from completely unthreading itself back through all the guides should you accidentally let it go. If you're not on grass or other soft, non-abrasive surface, you might want to have an old towel or hat to put the reel seat/reel into while threading the rod.

Pull all the leader material and some fly line out through the tiptop and tie on a fly using the appropriate knot (see knot section). Remember, fly line is relatively heavy. If you hold your rod upright and don't hold onto the

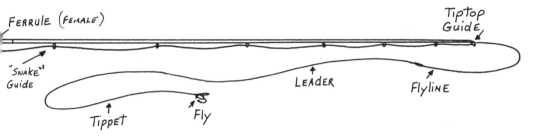

FERRULE (FEMALE)

Tiptop Guide

"SNAKE" Guide

LEADER

Flyline

Tippet

Fly

leader, the fly line will pull itself down and out of the guides, if there is no fly to stop it!

Check to make sure that you've passed the line through all the guides (its easy to miss one) and that the line moves freely through them. Now, grasp the rod by its handle to get a "feel" for its balance point and to become familiar with holding it in your hand.

A couple of additional pointers: Afterwards, when it comes time for you to disassemble your fly rod, don't bend the sections or twist them as you pull them apart. Instead, take a firm grip with one hand on each section, just short of arm's length, and pull each section *straight out,* and apart, to separate them. Wipe any moisture from the rod and put it back into the cloth sack it came with. The rod should also have a hard case. Most manufacturers supply either a plastic or aluminum tube to protect and store their products. The cloth sack and tubing protect the guides and rod from damage in your car's trunk and while transporting it. If your rod doesn't have one, it can either be purchased separately or easily made from a piece of PVC or ABS plastic tubing available at your local hardware or plumbing supply store.

Also, when slipping the rod either alone, or in its sack, into the tube, *surround the mouth of the tube* with your free hand. This cushions and protects the rod's guides from hitting the rim of the tube as the rod is inserted.

The fly line should be evenly rewound onto the reel under light tension and the reel wiped with a soft cloth. If the line was used in water during practice or after a day of fishing, I usually draw it through the folds of a towel to remove any grit or salt [water]. I'll then leave the reel out of its case for a day to let the moisture evaporate from the line and extend the life of the backing. Good equipment is worth taking care of.

Fly rod, reel, line and fly set up as discussed, you're now ready to *begin fly casting!*

Good friends on a fly-fishing adventure.▼

First Cast

*T*he act of fly casting is a beautiful thing to watch. The skilled angler artfully manipulates the line through the air with grace and form, delicately placing the fly in a predetermined location. The proper technique and conditions will reward the angler with a day filled with strikes, hookups and landed fish. Even days that aren't ideal offer the angler the opportunity to go out and attain a certain amount of pleasure and relaxation simply by fly casting, for a great deal of the satisfaction of fishing with a fly is drawn from fly casting itself. *Fly casting is fun!*

Let's begin with some basics. The fly reel is set up, as explained earlier, with 50 yards of backing, the fly line and a 7½–9 foot leader. The fly line and rod should be balanced with the correct fly line to match the rod's weight and preferably have a double taper or weight-forward line. Ideally, having someone who is a proficient fly caster instruct you on a one-to-one basis would be helpful, however, we are going to assume that this is not available, so we're going to teach ourselves.

Find an area that is 75–100 feet or so in length and at least 30–40 feet wide, relatively free of obstructions both on the ground and overhead. This can be in your backyard, the school yard or a park. Water, such as a pond or lake, would be nice but is not necessary. Instead, for your first lesson try to start early in the morning on the lawn or in a park while the grass is still wet from the previous night's dew. The grass is easier on the fly line than a

Hold the rod comfortably and naturally with the thumb along the top of the handle.

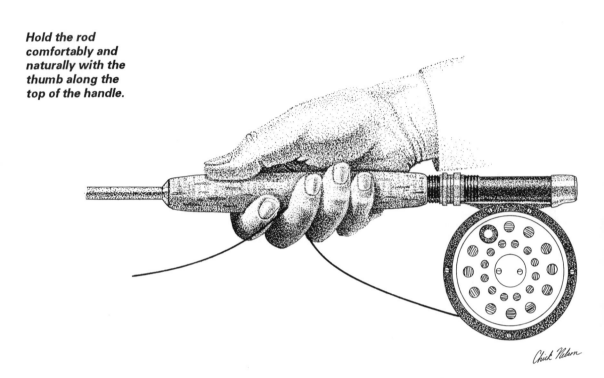

paved driveway and its wetness offers some resistance and added weight, as you will experience while on the water.

Position yourself about two-thirds of the way towards the back of the space in which you're going to practice, so that you have more length in front of you than behind. Once you've strung your leader and fly line through the rod's guides, attach either a fly, whose hook has been cut off with a pliers, or tie a small tuft of bright yarn onto the end of your leader. Practicing with the leader and fly (yarn) attached serves to duplicate on-stream conditions more closely. The leader helps "turn-over" the fly, while the yarn or fly gives you a more visible cue as to where your fly has landed.

Next, pull 10 or 15 feet of *fly line* off the reel, lay the rod/reel down on the ground and pull this line/leader out from the rod tip and lay it out in a straight line in front of you, in line with the rod. Pick up the rod, grip the handle

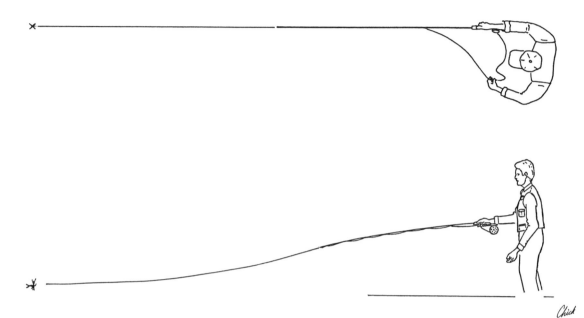

Chick

firmly, but comfortably as illustrated.

Position yourself so that you're turned slightly to the right (if you're right-handed), not square ahead, and sight down to your target area.

As we now know, the fly line itself will be cast. The leader, tippet and fly will be carried along by the fly line as opposed to the weight of a lure, bait or sinker pulling the line from a spinning or casting reel.

The rod and line will work in concert by the motion, power and timing of your cast. As you draw your rod upwards, the weight and resistance of the line and water will cause the rod to bend or "load." The rod, by its particular design and taper, is softer in the tip and becomes progressively stiffer towards the butt. The softer the tip and rod the slower the "action." Conversely, the stiffer the rod, the faster the action. Therefore, your timing will be different from one rod to another.

Start with the line and leader straight out in front, with all the slack removed. ▲

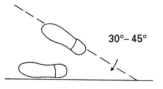

30°– 45°

Take a comfortable stand slightly off-center to your target

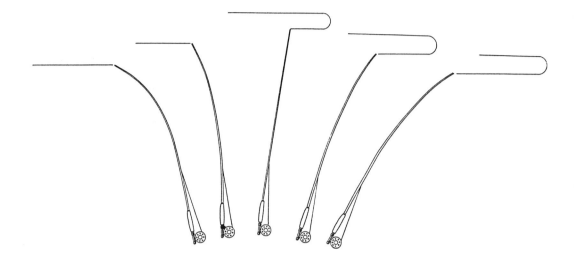

▲ *The fly rod flexes (loads) from the power of the cast then unloads its energy to throw the fly line forward.*

Start by gripping the rod with your right hand, the so-called "rod hand" (reverse these notes if left-handed). The grip, as illustrated, should be firm yet relaxed and comfortable. The fingers are wrapped around the cork handle with the thumb on top. This will enable you to more accurately control and power the forward cast, while at the same time "braking" the momentum of the rod on the back cast. The fly line should be gripped under your finger, or trapped between your finger and the handle. Your free hand is your "line hand," and will come into play later on. Now, with the fly line laid out in front of you and the fly rod pointed down, *remove any slack.* (The rod will not "load" until the slack is taken up.) Next, quickly and smoothly raise your hand and forearm upwards which will draw the line/leader off the ground (grass, water or whatever you're practicing on). As you raise the rod and lift the line over your right shoulder, *turn your head and watch as the line straightens out behind you.* You'll feel pressure on the rod as it is bending or "loading" against the weight of the fly line. As the line straightens out, the energy at the rod's tip is unloading, forcing the line backwards. This backwards motion of the line is the *back cast*.

As the fly line is forced backwards and upwards, the "loop" (the fly line's configuration as it unfolds) begins to unroll, beginning at the rod tip until it is straightened for its entire length, including the attached leader and fly. *At the point when the fly line is completely straight, with only a split second pause or drift, immediately begin your forward cast.* More than a slight pause and gravity starts to take over; the fly line will begin to drop and the success of the forward cast will lessen. Conversely, making the forward cast too early will result in "cracking the whip" which will often snap off your fly or result in putting a "wind knot" in your leader, thereby severely weakening it. The *proper timing,* however, will layout your line and leader just as straight as if you laid it out by hand. At first, don't try for distance but for a *smooth* power stroke in both the back cast and forward cast.

Turn your head and watch your fly line loop unroll to develop the proper timing for the forward cast.

COURTESY OF 3M/SCIENTIFIC ANGLERS

Now, all of this sounds a little intimidating, right? Well, no more so than the first time you stepped into a pair of roller-skates, sat behind the wheel of a car or anything else that required a modicum of learning or practice.

Let's do a little back-tracking now to better understand what you're trying to accomplish. An easy way to do this is to visualize yourself from a crosswise position to show the range of the rod's tip. The *rod's tip* is the key to success. The rod's tip not only controls the unleashing of the rod's energy but dictates the height and direction of the fly line.

Begin with the basic grip, the line coming off the reel, secured under your finger, all slack in the line removed. Your wrist and forearm are locked, your hand and arm are straight out in front, an extension of the fly rod. As you begin your back cast, the rod tip will travel rearwards, as shown, drawing the line upward.

From your imaginary crosswise viewpoint, imagine a clock face beside you. The rod's movement from back cast to forward cast remains in a range from 11 o'clock to 1 o'clock. You can see that by keeping the rod tip from dipping below the 1 o'clock position you are able to keep the fly line parallel to the ground. Envision the rod tip moving forward and back along the length of an overhead 180° straight line, almost as if you are running the rod tip along a horizontal clothesline overhead. In order to do this your casting motion must be a push–pull action, not a "waving" of the rod back and forth with the elbow fixed in one position, acting as a pivot. *Push* the rod *forward*, not down, and slightly extend the arm forward at the elbow. The movement of the *casting stroke* is not an overhand stroke but a

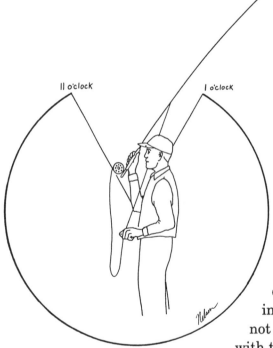

II o'clock   I o'clock

The rod tip's range is from 11 o'clock to 1 o'clock

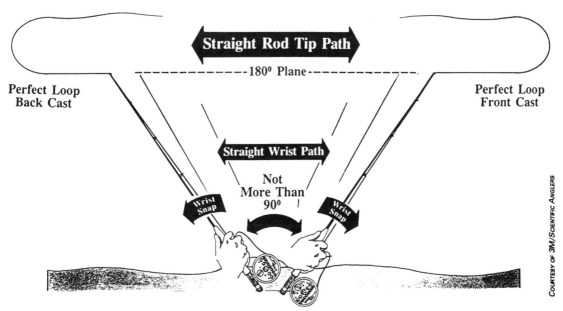

The basic casting stroke should be fluid yet should strive for straight, direct line movements along a flat line for the most efficient energy transfer.

push ahead and *forward* motion, the hand moving from front to back in a nearly straight line, with a slight upward lift, stopping at 1 o'clock. On the back cast, again *pull* the rod back, extending the arm and stabbing the rod backward. *Watch your fly line/leader's loop unroll* and complete the forward cast. Don't wave the rod or you'll wave the tip. The tip then moves in an arc—and where the tip goes, so goes the line creating a wider, less efficient loop.

Relax...if the first cast didn't work out don't get frustrated. Try it again. Most likely if there was a problem it was somewhere between the end of the back cast and the forward cast. Allow the back cast loop to *completely* unroll. When you begin the forward cast, don't try to bash it. The timing and smooth transition of the accelerating power of the forward cast and pressure on the line will make the cast successful.

Back Cast

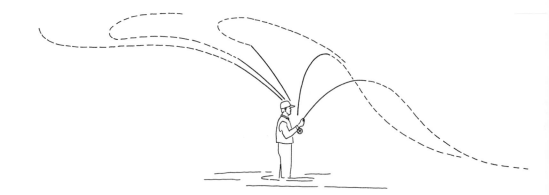

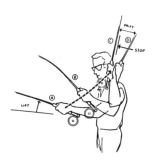

▲ In the casting stroke the hand moves from front to back in a nearly straight line with a slight upward lift, stoping at 1 o'clock. Open the wrist slightly and allow the rod to drift back. ▼

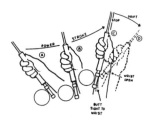

Now, let's try another cast. This time you can either keep the fly line trapped between the fingers or rod grip as before or grasp it with you free hand, allowing the hand to follow the rod's movements. Your line is out in front, grip is firm yet comfortable, all slack in the line is removed. Your stance should be relaxed with your left foot pointed toward your intended target, body facing just slightly right helping to clear the fly line from your body. You'll want your wrist to remain rigid, for if you flex or bend it prematurely, you will aggravate the arc and drop your rod tip, and consequently your line. Remember, the hand, wrist and forearm should act as an extension of the rod. Your movements should be quick and firm, adding power to your "stroke" as the rod is lifted upward. Think "rod tip." Believe it or not, thinking of where and at what attitude the rod tip is, brings the other subconscious motions of your casting arm into play.

There is one aspect of the transition between the back cast and the forward cast that needs to be mentioned, and that is the separation of the two casting planes. This generally happens more naturally in the beginner than in the intermediate fly caster, probably because with all that is going on the novice tends to unconsciously open or twist his or her wrist to the right thus moving the rod tip in a *slightly* oval path, when viewed from above. If you did not open the wrist slightly, but instead rigidly moved the rod back and forth in exactly the same plane, your line and leader are prone to hit the rod, as the unrolling portion of the loop comes in contact with the part already extended, thus destroying the cast.

This problem can be easily eliminated by separating the two casting planes. Keep the forward casting plan vertical and the back casting plane tipped *slightly* off vertical, and to the right by a slight twist of the wrist. Consider this if you're having a problem with the line running into your rod on the forward cast.

Okay...lift the rod smoothly, accelerating and adding power as the line straightens out. *Turn your head to watch your line straighten out behind you and to time at what point to begin your forward cast.* Keep the rod tip up as you "push" it backwards, the tip sliding along as if running along that invisible clothesline suspended in the air. At 1 o'clock," extend your arm and "stab" the rod up and back.

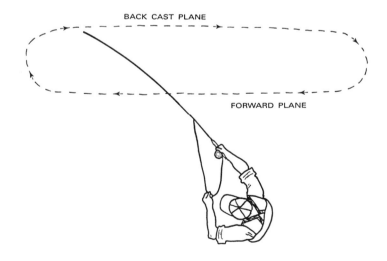

BACK CAST PLANE

FORWARD PLANE

Separate the forward and backward casting planes by tipping the backcast slightly off vertical

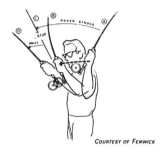

▲ From the 1 o'clock position, the forward stroke should move the hand in a nearly straight line with a slight overhand motion. Gradually closing the wrist and stopping the rod at the 11 o'clock position. ▼

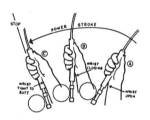

After the rod is stopped, you can allow your wrist to open *slightly* as the line drifts backwards. Now, just as the line begins to reach its most rearward extension, pause for a fraction of a second to *allow the line to straighten completely* but not fall, then begin your forward power stroke, again smoothly and in control, letting the rod do the work. The line's weight will "load" the rod. The flexing of the rod will transfer the energy of the forward cast to the rod's tip.

A major temptation when learning is to overpower the forward stroke, to "muscle" it and throw it forward. Wrong! R-E-L-A-X. Use the same steady, *progressive* power stroke in the forward cast as in the back cast. Watch for the formation of a tight loop, which is the most effective because it minimizes the line's wind resistance.

As you complete your forward cast and as the fly line straightens out in front, add a slight snap or "squeeze" to your grip. You can now flex/bend the wrist to create the "snap" as you lower the rod tip,

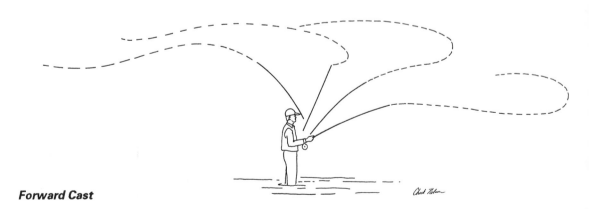

Forward Cast

thereby letting the line drop lightly and parallel to the ground. The fly or yarn tied to the leader's end should *turn over* (that is, completely unfurl as the forward loop unrolls) and land gently in the approximate area to which it was cast. The snap or squeeze correlates to your visualizing and feeling what your rod tip is doing to *drive* the fly line cleanly and fluidly forward with enough energy transfer to unroll the fly line loop completely. You will know when you do it, and once you "feel" the snap/squeeze you'll be able to control each cast.

Vary the line length out from the reel. Experiment. Fifteen feet of fly line instead of twenty is more comfortable for the first few casts. Then *gradually* lengthen it to twenty or twenty-five feet, but *don't rush it!* We'd all like to cast fifteen or twenty *yards* the first day, but like any sport, practice is what makes perfect, as they say.

Allow the back cast's loop to completely unroll before beginning the forward cast. ▼

▲ *The proper execution of the forward cast forms a tight, efficient casting loop.*

In both the forward and back cast be alert to the feel of the constant pressure of the fly line loading and unloading the rod. Keep this connection in mind. The *rod* develops the power; the *rod tip* controls the power. Maintain that mental and physical connection between you, the rod, and line. Be aware and keep this constant line pressure—the connection. Lose it and lose the potential for a great cast. Control the line, pace your timing, and *don't wave* the rod. Mentally form a picture of what the line and rod tip are doing both while casting *and while not casting*. Visualization and mental practice help to put the body in touch with what it needs to do to coordinate the proper actions.

Avoid excessive "false casting" when actually fishing. This preparatory movement, making repetitive forward and back casts without actually touching the water, is useful in drying out a fly, but as long as the fly is out of the water it won't catch any fish. Also, wet flies and nymphs are meant to quickly sink upon hitting the water, and excessive false casts defeat the purpose. Two or three false casts are usually sufficient to line up the target zone, estimate its distance, or change direction. Don't over do it.

Practice for 15–20 minutes or for a relatively short duration for the first few sessions rather than for one "no pain–no gain" session. Shorter, more frequent practices, develop better technique than those that can be obtained from fatigued, newly developing muscles.

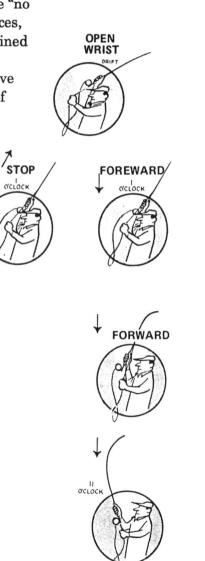

A few other points should be noted that can improve and accelerate your learning and lessen the chance of frustration early on: If someone is available to help you cast, you'd be wise to consider if they'd be more of a help than a hindrance (*sometimes,* spouses make poor teachers since they can add undo pressure if your progress isn't up to what is expected). Don't be intimidated. *You can learn to fly cast by yourself!* Practice when you're fresh and relaxed. Also, if you can get out earlier in the day, practice fields, school yards and parks are generally less crowded and afford a much more relaxed atmosphere. In the beginning, as you're learning, remember to *turn and look behind you as you back cast,* first obviously to avoid any overhead obstacles such as trees, power lines and the like, but also to watch your line, keeping it from dropping, and to develop the proper timing for the perfect forward cast. Bright colored fly lines are an aid in this regard.

Keep your back cast high. Don't let your rod stop past the 1–1:30 o'clock position.

Courtesy of Fenwick

Slapping the water 'fore and aft and breaking off hook tips on rocks behind you are not in your best interest. Work on your *timing*—make your forward cast too soon and you'll crack the whip (and snap off your fly!). Make the forward cast too soon and your rod won't *load* (flex) and therefore you'll run out of the very power necessary to propel it forward. Make your forward cast too late and not only will you drop your line via gravity, but again you'll lose the *load* (energy) of the rod—timing in fly casting, as in life, is everything.

Specialized Casts

As you progress and perfect the basic cast, you'll come to realize that there will be times when prevailing conditions will necessitate a divergence from the basic to a specialized cast to fit the circumstance at hand. I include these so that this book will grow with you, but don't feel obligated or pressured into feeling that you need to learn these right away. You will do quite well catching fish in a variety of conditions with the basic cast and you should be proficient and comfortable with it *before* attempting to move on. At that point, the addition of one of the specialized casting techniques to your repertoire will add to the fun!

The basic forward cast is just that. It is the foundation for other more complex techniques. Under certain fishing conditions, however, it will often be necessary to cast without sufficient clearance behind you, or to add additional drag-free drift to your fly, or to extend additional line to a distant rising fish.

Let's talk about a few of these techniques:

▌Roll Cast

Inevitably there will be times, when at streamside or lakeside, when you will not have sufficient clearance behind you to make a proper aerial back cast—a low bank, trees, bushes and the like would interfere with your back cast—therefore you'll need to keep your fly line in front of you.

To *roll cast,* begin with sufficient line in the water in front of you. A double taper fly line works best for this technique. The line, laying in the water with its related tension, is what makes this technique work. Slowly raise your rod and arm up and back, drawing the line towards you and incline the rod slightly over your right shoulder. Just as the rod and line are approaching the vertical position, allow the line to fall back over your shoulder. Hesitate momentarily to give the water a chance to get a grip on the line (its friction will load the rod). Then, make a *forward* and *downward* roll cast. The rod tip's energy will draw and power the line in a large loop and unroll the line and fly out ahead of you. A few practice casts, adjusting and experimenting with the position of the line as it approaches your elbow, prior to the power being applied to the cast, will soon make you an expert. Remember, however, that this technique does need to be practiced with your fly line *on the water* for it to work.

Rod is raised just past the vertical position. Power is applied, rolling the line out to the target area. ▼

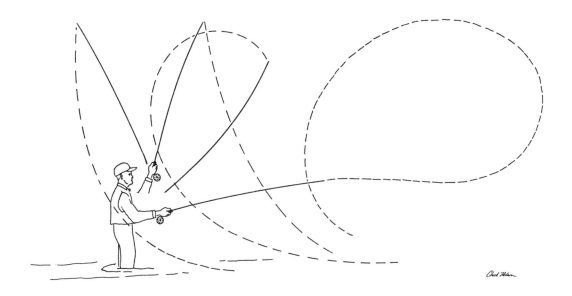

A variation of this technique involves using the roll cast to pull up a sunken line. Thus applied, this is called a **roll cast pickup.** To execute the roll cast pickup, begin as you would the roll cast as outlined earlier but this time point the rod tip higher and roll the line *above the water.* As the line straightens out in the air, draw the rod back and cast up and back as you would in a normal back cast.

A Tower or Steeple cast is useful where trees, high banks or other obstructions impede a more horizontal back cast.

∎ Tower or Steeple Cast

There are two useful casts that are variations of the basic front and back cast, used when there isn't sufficient clearance behind you to utilize the traditional back cast. The first is called, among other things, a *Tower cast* or *Steeple cast.* To make a Steeple cast, the rod and line plane are skewed so that the rod begins at a more downward angle and is draw back and *up*, stopping at the 12 o'clock position. As you look back over your shoulder to observe your fly line, you should imagine, if you will, a tall steeple, and the back cast should throw the line at an angle to clear the steeple, or in actuality, the tree or bank you need to clear.

∎ Side or Lateral Cast

An alternate cast is the *side* or *lateral cast.* Again, employed when back clearance is limited, and when you need to "go under the wind" or place your fly low over the water to land under some shady, low-hanging branches. It's also useful in "stalking" still water, at close range, when the motion or shadow of your overhead rod may spook a fish. Essentially, this is the basic cast executed with a *sidearm* or *lateral* motion and the rod tilted down to one side. This cast seems to develop almost automatically in one form or another as you observe surrounding conditions and attain proficiency and confidence in your abilities.

∎ Slack Cast

Sometimes called the serpentine, snake cast or S-cast, the slack cast is very useful when additional drift is needed when casting across or downstream or similar conditions. Just as the forward cast is completed and the fly line is dropping towards the water, the rod is given a series of quick short, side-to-side shakes, the rod tip transfers the action to the line, and the line lands on the water in a series of undulating curves. This intentional *slack* serves to add a few seconds to the fly's drift, giving the fish time to strike before drag sets in and the line pulls the fly.

Snake Cast: Move the rod tip side-to-side to create a controlled amount of slack and extend the fly's drag-free drift. ▼

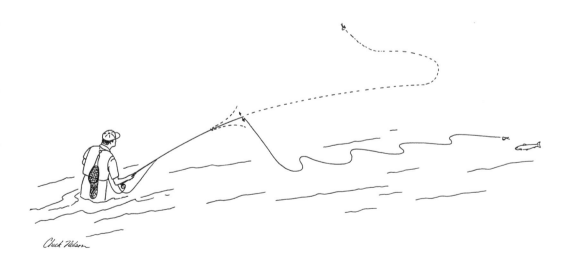

■ Parachute Cast

As the name would imply, implementation of the parachute cast permits the fly to alight on the water very softly. This can be very useful in quiet waters where a normal cast would spook your fish.

To make a parachute cast, cast as usual, possibly extending line and/or changing direction so that your fly drops just ahead or within striking distance to drift pass your fish. As you complete the forward power cast, give the rod a short, quick jerk backwards to stop the line, then immediately lower the rod. This action allows the fly to gently *float* the last foot or two down onto the water's surface with hardly a ripple.

Using a reach cast for a straight upstream presentation will prevent the fly line from floating over the fish and spooking it. ▼

COURTESY OF 3M/SCIENTIFIC ANGLERS

■ Splat Cast

There are times when bass fishing or perhaps when drifting down a swift river and casting to the water along the banks, when it is necessary to call immediate attention to your fly, imitating a larger "bug" or *terrestrial* that has dropped into the water. For this, we call upon the *splat* cast. To do so, make your forward cast, but apply slightly more power than usual. As the leader is about to turn over, pull the rod tip toward you, slapping the fly onto the water. Don't over do it, but land the fly with enough of a "splat" to imitate a dropping bug.

■ Reach Cast

There will be occasions, when either casting dry-flies or nymphs upstream or to a pocket on the side of a boulder, when you either don't want to "line" a fish or need to drop the fly to the side of your target area. By lining a fish, I mean casting straight upstream and dropping your fly line on the water directly over the fish, thereby spooking it prior to the fly floating downstream to present itself. In these situations a *reach cast* is useful, even essential.

Cast as usual, extending line if necessary, then just as you make the forward cast and your line is unrolling forward, *move the rod tip to either the right or left.* The fly will continue in the intended direction, but the fly line will extend at an angle from the rod tip to the fly, rather than in a straight line. This same technique will also allow you to place your fly *around* an obstacle.

■ Extend Cast/Shooting Line

As you gain proficiency in handling both rod and line, you eventually want to increase the distance of your casts. To do so, pull off an extra 6–8' of line from the reel, and let it drop loosely, uncoiled at your feet. Hold your rod in your rod hand as usual. Now, instead of holding and trapping the line with your right index finger, take hold of it with your left index finger and thumb where the reel is attached to the rod. As you raise the rod for the back cast, bring your left hand up *along with the rod.* After a false cast or two, to prepare yourself and feel the pressure or pull on the line, make your forward cast. Subtly add a little extra *progressive* power to the forward cast. Then, adding a squeezing wrist snap just as the fly line unfurls, and with the rod tip positioned slightly higher than usual, release the line through an "o" formed by your thumb and index finger, maintaining line control with your fingertips. If you time your release to the point of the transfer of energy, the fly line will easily withdraw the slack line from the loose coils at your feet and "shoot" the extra line. It takes a little practice, and timing is crucial, but it's a fun and practical way to cover increased distances and *shoot* under overhanging bushes and tree limbs.

■ Double Haul Cast

This specialized cast may sound relatively simple, but its timing needs to be perfected by frequent practice before it's effective. The double haul can greatly increase your distance casting, help bust through the wind, and is a valuable tool in casting highly air-resistant bass bugs or larger saltwater streamers.

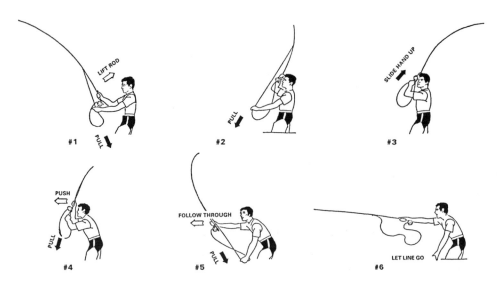

▲ A double haul increases line speed for longer casts and additional power to help bust through the wind.

Begin by grasping the fly line with the non-rod hand and hold it between the thumb and forefinger at a point just below the stripping guide. As you raise the rod for the back cast, begin to pull down on the line. Begin slowly, then accelerate the speed of the pull as you raise the rod. As the fly rod is lifted (and stopped) at the 12 o'clock position, and the back cast rolls out, you'll feel the pressure/pull on the fly line, as the rod is under full load of the line. *Allow your line hand to travel back up to the butt of the rod, while still holding onto the fly line.*

At the completion of the back cast, allow the rod to drift back to the 1 o'clock position. Begin the forward cast, blending one motion into the next. Both your line hand and rod hand will be close together at this point. Begin to quickly pull the fly line so that as you stop the rod at the 11 o'clock position, a final tug is made. (This second vigorous tug is a long one, pulling the line down below your waist.) Release the line, lowering the rod tip to minimize any friction, maximize the distance, and to throw the line low and parallel to the water, under the wind. As you gain experience you can strip out a half a dozen yards of fly line and shoot it out on the completion and release of the second (double) "haul."

Both the tug on the back cast and the forward cast need to be made *precisely* at the moment the rod is stopped at the 1 o'clock and 11 o'clock positions. *Timing is the key*.

"✳@?#!..." Wind

There will inevitably be times when you're at your favorite water and the wind comes up. We're not talking about an occasional breeze whose slight disturbance of the water can actually help shield your silhouette from a fish, but wind—strong blowing air. You have but two choices: wait it out or deal with it. Adjusting to it obviously saves the day, so let's look at our options.

Given a choice, wind at your back is better than in your face, if it works out that way. A "tail wind" will affect your back cast, but making a tighter casting loop, by limiting the range of movement to a shorter, brisker stroke, will help to keep the line from collapsing. Change the angle of the back cast so it is at a lower angle than usual in order to avoid bucking the wind head-on. Try to use the wind to your advantage by raising the forward cast's angle somewhat to have the wind assist the delivery of the line and fly. Make your forward cast with a minimal amount of false casting to decrease the likelihood of tangling your line, since a tail wind will assist your forward cast anyway.

A "head wind" offers its own set of problems, as it will impede the smooth unrolling of your fly line and leader. As with the back cast above, you will need to make your forward cast's loop as small as possible to efficiently cut through the wind. Using a double-haul to get line speed and power into your cast can help. The added forward density of either a weight-forward line, combined with a

Wind...the curse of the fly-fisher. Casting a virtually weightless fly on a thick, wind-resistant fly line in the wind can be an exercise in frustration unless you make some changes.

stiffer leader will also help. You could switch to a sink-tip line and try fishing wets/nymphs or, more radically, move to a heavier rod/line weight to punch through the wind. Smaller, less bushy flies, help some but I've found that when the wind disturbs the water surface (and the fish's ability to see what is floating on top), I tend to stick with a fly large enough for the fish to see. Also remember that the wind will blow 'hoppers, beetles and other terrestrials into the water. Therefore, casting one of these larger flies close to a bank will likely draw a strike. Side-casts, in which the rod is held parallel to the water and at a lower angle than on the forward cast, will keep your line low over the water and "under the wind," and can be effective, depending on the direction and intensity of the wind.

I remember one day on Montana's Madison River where there were 30+mph gusts that nearly had me heading back to the car, but I was determined to stay, having come so far to fish this water. I was able to get into a decent number of fish by using a combination of things that lessened the wind's impact.

For one, I moved to a section of the river where the direction of the wind worked to my advantage. I also kept my casts shorter, making the line easier to control, knowing that I could approach each lie a little closer since the wind obscured the fish's vision through the water's surface. When possible I'd time my casts between gusts and kept my casts low. I also would occasionally let the wind pick up my line and let the leader "dap" the fly on and off the water, as if a caddisfly was fluttering and dropping her eggs. I can't say it was the most fun I've ever had fishing, but you can meet the challenge and fool enough fish to make the day worthwhile.

If you can't change the circumstances, then change your technique and approach the situation from another angle...there's more than one way to skin a *"cat" fish!*

ON THE WATER TECHNIQUES

Reading The Water 3

*I*t **has been said** that 10% of the flymen catch 90% of the fish. Conversely, the other 90% of the fishermen catch only 10% of the *available* fish.........well, this may be a bit over-stated but, truly, the minority of fishermen take a majority of the fish *and* the largest fish. To successfully fish is to hunt for and find where there are fish. The environment may vary by species but the basic premises remain the same: *RULE #1: Never fish on or over vacant water!*

Obviously, not all running waters are the same nor are they uniform throughout their length. Depending on its size, moving water may be called a brook, a creek, a stream or a river and, of course, there are the still waters: ponds, reservoirs, lakes, and the like. The water will vary depending on the time of the year and amount of runoff, the gradient or drop per mile, the basic nature of the sub-surface, etc. Rivers and streams, for instance, may contain steep narrow sections, wider flatter areas, ledges, boulders, submerged logs, etc., all influencing its flow and providing sections of fast water, slow water, runs, riffles, pocket-water and everything in between. Lakes and other still water meanwhile provide varying types of cover and environments in the form of weedbeds, lily pads, submerged and/or fallen trees, perhaps old riverbed channels in man-made impoundments, inlet and/or outlet streams, thermoclines (temperature stratifications), and the like.

As a fly-fisher, you can have the finest equipment, the best tied flies and the perfect cast, but unless you place your offering where the fish are most likely to be, then the results are going to be far less than satisfying. *You can't catch what ain't there.* (RULE #1) So, let's look at where we can find fish.

Fish, like most wild things, are predators, as was man before he learned to cultivate his own food. Their needs are basic: survival based on an environment suitable to their metabolism and energy retention, protection from predators, and a steady source of food for sustenance. A stream or still water environment must provide for all the above for it to be viable.

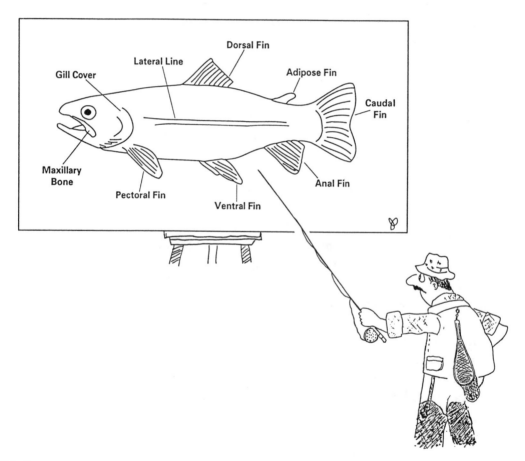

... Fish "Facts"

Lies

Let's begin with where to find fish—their *lies*. Trout in moving water generally hold in one position in the current…the so-called *lie*. There are four basic types of "lies" (five if you include the size of the fish that you told your friends you caught—but that's a different kind of lie!) There are *holding lies, sheltering lies, feeding lies* and *prime lies*.

A **Holding lie** is just that. No creature can constantly burn its energy at a high rate without relief, thus protection from strong/swift currents is a high priority. A holding lie is a station which offers mitigation from the strongest current; a place to conserve energy with some measure of protection, security and occasional food.

Protection from the current and from predators is the highest priority and fish will, for a time, sacrifice feeding and other environmental conditions in order to ensure their basic survival. Various birds, other fish at times, an assortment of four-legged animals and, of course, man are all natural enemies. To protect themselves from these dangers, trout will scoot for cover into a *sheltering lie*.

Sheltering lies provide cover, concealment and relief from the swiftest currents. Most trout are well-suited for the task of concealment by Mother Nature. Their backs are generally dark in color and are mottled to blend in with the stream bottoms, with lighter bellies to blend against the surface, when seen from below. Sheltering lies offer protection and are where trout and other fish go when threatened. They can scoot to these predetermined locations in a flash. An undercut bank, ledge, weedbed, pocket below a sunken log, a deep shaded area beneath a bush or tree, or the deepest recesses of the stream-bottom—all can afford the sanctuary necessary to provide relief. Holding or resting in a sheltered lie provides the comfort zone that the name implies: the water temperature, oxygen level, current rate and flow provide the conditions necessary for a regathering of strength and energy.

Courtesy of 3M/Scientific Anglers

▲ *Trout go to sheltering lies for protection when they are spooked or hooked. Unlike feeding lies, there is no funnel effect around sheltering lies and so they offer little or no food.*

Our finned quarry must also be able to operate in relative comfort. To a fish, be it trout, salmon, bass, etc., this may mean different things. Water temperature is an important consideration as fish are cold-blooded creatures and, as such, cannot regulate their internal body temperature. The colder the water, the slower their metabolism and therefore the slower their reaction time. Conversely, within safe limits, the warmer waters provide a higher metabolic rate, more active fish (due, in part, also to increased insect activity), higher consumption of energy and a greater need to feed. Different species have different ideal temperature ranges. The chart below gives the basic parameters.

Species	Preferred Temperature Range
Rainbow Trout	55–65°F
Brown Trout	55–62°F
Brook Trout	55–63°F
Smallmouth Bass	55–75°F
Largemouth Bass	60–80°F

Related to the comfort factor is the need to maintain energy. Food is, therefore, another major consideration. If a fish is secure in his environment, it will naturally seek to find a reliable source of food to replenish itself. If it is to survive, however, it must obtain greater energy from the food than that necessary to take it. While fish may be found in swift waters, they are not constantly in the heaviest flow. They will find a location, a *station*, that moderates the balance of energy expended for food supply obtained. This can be accomplished in a variety of ways. For one, the science of water hydraulics shows us that the water speed is not constant. In the water column, the flow is swiftest in its center and slower on the sides and bottom caused by the friction and interaction with the stream bottom and banks. These areas are further broken up into specific slower areas of stream flow by rock formations, submerged debris, depressions in the streambed and other underwater obstructions. All of these offer a place, albeit small, that offer some protection and relief from the

Feeding lies occur in shallow sections of the stream. One very good place for a feeding lie is where the current forms a funnel effect between obstructions. Fish hold just downstream from these spots where food organisms concentrate.

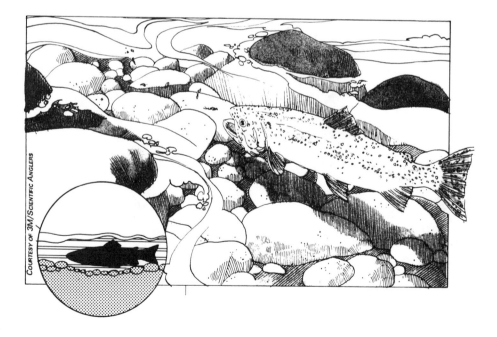

COURTESY OF 3M/SCIENTIFIC ANGLERS

Trout in moving water will seek conditions that offer either relief from the current, security or food. Note typical areas that present these conditions either individually or simultaneously; sides, front and rear of boulders, below deadfalls, inlets of springs, below oxygenated riffles, under-cut banks, etc. ▼

incessant flow that passes by. Therefore, current flows that funnel tidbits of subaquatic insects, weedbeds that serve as nurseries for the various stages of insect life, areas of low-flow where a fish can forage for other baitfish or immature fish and/or crustaceans provide the ideal *feeding lie*.

Feeding lies are lanes and seams that provide the avenues where a steady supply of surface and subsurface morsels are filtered into the fish's world and fish will go to these areas to actively feed. These can be areas underlying trees or bushes where bugs are regularly blown into the water, areas where the surface film carries downstream dead or dying, flying or egg-laying insects, or subsurface channels that funnel the streamborn nymphs and larvae into a fish's path.

Combine all of the above with the need for an oxygenated water supply, which is diminished as water temperature rises, and fish's increased need as energy is expended,

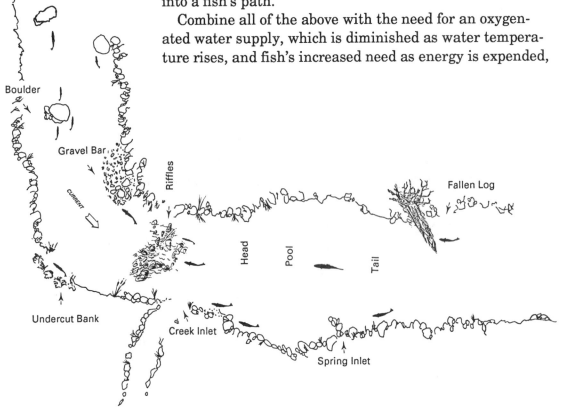

Boulder

Gravel Bar

Riffles

current

Fallen Log

Head

Pool

Tail

Undercut Bank

Creek Inlet

Spring Inlet

and we come up with almost an infinite number of variables for the perfect spot to *place that fly!*

Obviously, an area that provides all of the above criteria would be considered *prime,* for here our finned aquavore would feel unthreatened by the world around it, as it would have an adequate oxygen supply, would not have to fin unnecessarily hard, and would have a ready food supply. These ideal or *prime lies* not only exist but provide the biggest, and in some cases the most fish, and season-upon-season can give the angler who discovers them continual pleasure! When a fish is taken from such a lie (and hopefully released to swim again for your or someone else's pleasure), that lie will soon be occupied by another for the conditions it presents. Often, these lies are small enough only for one fish, but sometimes can be occupied by a handful.

Prime lies are sometimes readily apparent to the trained eye, sometimes not. Prime lies have several things in common simultaneously: sufficient depth or cover to offer protection, a steady flow of water to bring the food supply to the fish, and an obstruction to slow or break the water's flow. Boulders, visible at the water's surface or evidenced by the water's disturbance above it, a fallen tree or log jutting from a streambank, a series of large rocks with pockets between them or the convergence of fast deep water joined by a slower inlet stream offer the depth, food supply and ideal current to enable our fish to dine, in comfort, at will. More often than not these prime lies, though more visible with our increased ability to read the water, may not always be readily accessible either from the bank or by wading. Often, the jumbled currents and counter-currents, caused and formed by the same conditions that provide the prime lie, make it exceedingly difficult to make a drag-free cast long enough to do us any good. But that is the fun and challenge of fly-fishing and what makes it sporting, for how long would these lies remain "prime" if man became the major predator?

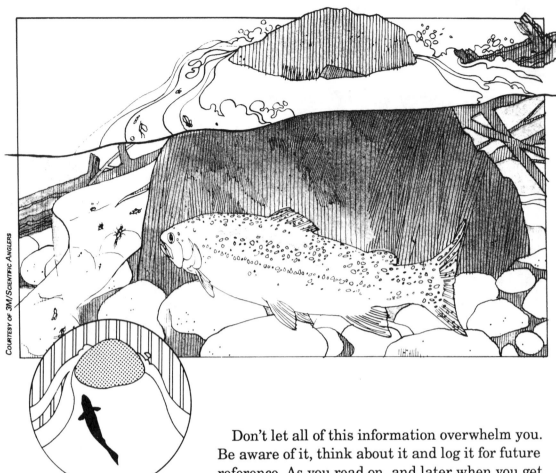

▲ *A prime lie is in deeper water than a feeding lie. It offers the fish both food and shelter.*

Don't let all of this information overwhelm you. Be aware of it, think about it and log it for future reference. As you read on, and later when you get to the water, this will become perfectly logical. As you mentally review your various successes, count how many of the aforementioned conditions were present when you get that strike or saw that rise. It will soon become a subconscious study as you scan the water. This will separate you from the "chuck and chance it" angler and greatly add to the anticipation and excitement of each cast.

Water Types

Running water, be it a small creek or a large river, will generally not be uniform throughout its length, but will be broken up into a number of water types, depending on its volume, velocity and obstructions over which it must pass. Moving water, for instance, will reveal some of its subsurface features by telegraphing these upwards to the surface. As a new fly-fisher you should be familiar with what to expect from these. Lakes and other still waters have their own characteristics and will be covered later on.

Riffles are areas of fast, broken water, scattered throughout the stream course. They are usually relatively shallow water, running over a bed of rocks and small boulders, some of which may be visible on the surface. The broken subsurface serves to thoroughly mix and oxygenate the water giving it life for the fish and providing a rich aquatic nursery for mayfly and stonefly nymphs as well as caddis larvae and other insect life.

Prime water in the riffle area is where, circumstances permitting, there is an occasional large boulder or other obstruction *interspersed with somewhat deeper water to provide shelter* and space for larger fish. Slick water in and among riffled water can belie a shelf or ledge, or a depression which can hold larger fish. Be observant for this condition. Generally, food-rich riffled waters hold a good number of fish, although not always the largest in the stream because of the limitation of sizeable sheltered water, but they are fun to fish. Thoroughly work its corners, edges and seams. Riffle water is a good bet when water temperatures rise because it provides life-giving oxygen depleted in the water's warmer, slower sections.

Fast-current riffles are shallow, even-bottomed sections of streams that have little or no white water. ▼

COURTESY OF 3M/SCIENTIFIC ANGLERS

▲ *Rock Creek:
working the prime
water below a set
of riffles.*

Runs are long stretches of relatively smooth water that
are often located between sets of riffles. Generally, they
are shallower at their "head," deeper through their length,
and either spill into a larger, deeper pool or shallow-out in
their tailout section prior to being lifting into the next
riffle. Straight runs can have deceptively strong waterflow.
If a run meanders, it tends to have deeper, swifter water
and *undercut banks on its outside edge* and slower, shallower water with accompanying gravel bars on the inside
of the bend. Consider these undercut banks as you work
your way upstream. The eroded banks of a stream or the
outside bend of a spring creek provide a sanctuary that
offers shelter, food and security—*a prime lie*. Given sufficient depth of a foot or more and/or cover provided by
roots, shade, shrubbery, or indentations and the like,
undercut banks and ledges offer security and therefore
sanctuary. They also provide a second primary need—food.
In moving water fish can eye drifting insects and baitfish

from their safe harbor, intercepting various aquatic insects as they migrate towards shore and dine on terrestrials that unwillingly drop from shoreline greenery. Combine these two important basic needs with protection from the drain of fighting a heavy current and we must assume that this is prime water, more often than not, and needs to be carefully and thoroughly fished.

Fishing the banks and undercut ledges requires a careful, quiet approach. This is even more important in a clear, slow moving meadow stream or spring creek where even the vibration of your foot-fall can alert wary trout to your presence. Approach the water slowly, keeping a low silhouette. It is not uncommon to stalk your quarry on all fours on particularly tricky water as you get into position. Stay well back from the water and cast so your fly lands *tight* to the bank. Your quarry will be close to the stream-side vegetation or in the undercut / indentation, therefore only an accurate cast will place your fly into its cone of

Success! ▼

vision. Likewise, if you're drifting a wet-fly or streamer, it should drift and/or begin its swing close to the suspected lie to be effective.

The gravel bars formed by the deposition of the stream gravels in high water on the *inside bends* are pleasant areas to walk/wade as you probe the irregularities of the stream's course. They usually offer convenient access to the water and unobstructed casting room. Depending on a stream's velocity and width, gravel bars can also provide a ready approach to otherwise difficult casting to the opposite shore's prime water.

During my earlier life, when gold prospecting proceeded my fly-fishing days, I'd often don a diver's facemask, walk to the head of a long run, and drift face-down exploring the underwater world. I'd surprise and observe countless trout as I drifted along downstream, peeking around and over the river bottom's rocks and depressions, always fascinated as to how many fish there were swimming about.

Runs offer trout a number of advantages. The streambed, unless unusually smooth, offers a number of areas where a fish can fin almost effortlessly, given the friction and slower water at the bottom of the water column. Minor depressions in the bottom offer further protection from the current as well as an ideal vantage point to view food-stuff drifting overhead. The deeper water offers a larger measure of protection from predation than does the more shallow riffle and will often hold larger fish that have outgrown the riffle area. Runs offer a suitable balance of oxygen and cooler temperatures as well as a holding area for crayfish, sculpin, fingerlings and other baitfish so preferred by larger fish.

I'd be remiss if I omitted an incident that happened a few years ago to my wife and me in a prime run on a magnificent Idaho stream. We had been fishing most of the day and doing some vacation filming with our videocamera. I had convinced Nancy to climb down the steep streambank one more time to fish this particular

section. She did so, somewhat reluctantly, having already
had her fill that day of fat, 12–14 inch cutthroat trout. She
proceeded to catch, land and release a half dozen fish in
the next half hour but was doing it more to satisfy me
than herself. She was anxious to call it a day when she
hooked into a smallish Rainbow which was frantically
trying to escape. Eyeing this through the lens of the
camcorder's viewfinder, I could see a slight bend in her
5 weight rod. She was saying something to the effect of,
"Okay, this is it—I'm tired—tomorrow's another day."
Suddenly, the rod arched violently. Her attention instantly
returned to her fish and, shocked back into reality, she
was shouting to me in disbelief that a monster fish had his
"lips" around her fish, mid-body. This confrontation lasted
no more than 4–5 seconds, but I filmed the whole event.

*Prime water means prime
fish — Oregon 'Bow.* ▼

The larger fish was never "hooked," as the smaller fish was wearing the hook in its lip, but the smaller fish was cut almost in half. From best we can figure, the struggling smaller fish had dredged up a cannibalistic brown trout weighing perhaps six to eight pounds for which this river is famous. Her landing the latter fish was never very important to me but capturing the unusual event on video and my wife's surprise, excitement, joy, shock and disbelief was worth a dozen landed fish. She has now committed herself to seeking out a similar beauty, this time hooked to her fly, when we return to this fantastic river. The point is, *prime runs hold prime fish.*

Fishing a long run presents a number of challenges because, although at first there is a sameness to the look of a run, there can be quite a diversity and variety of conditions and opportunities present. Depending on the season, time of day, etc., a good run will present excellent dry-fly fishing through most of the head and tailout areas, along with select areas in its mid-section. A well-drifted dry can be viewed from below by a number of fish, one of which is bound to drift upwards to inspect and/or strike at the proper fly. The head of the run, or of a pool, just *below*

Rapids have uneven bottoms, large boulders and deep turbulent waters.

a riffle is excellent for both dry and wet-fly presentations as the combination of insect life and oxygenated water will lure the fish to it. There are, however, some inherent problems presenting a fly in this area. Tumbling water can quickly drown a dry-fly, while at the same time the amount of "air" in the water will make if difficult to sink a wet-fly quickly enough to reach the depth of the holding fish. Conversely, the jumbled surface of the swift, broken water at the run's head can forgive a sloppy, heavy-handed presentation...so, there is balance. Adjust your presentation accordingly. A heavily dressed (fully hackled) dry-fly will float better and longer than a sparsely tied one. Tuck-cast a wet-fly or nymph so that it hits the water hard and sinks and reaches the fish's level quickly. Remember to tend your line to maintain the correct line tension to enable you to detect the strike and react to it prior to the fish spitting out the phony.

The *mid-run*, where the water level is often deepest, is best fished wet, unless a hatch is on and rises are evident. A well-placed, drag-free, drifted nymph, emerger or wet, played with a strike-indicator affixed at the proper depth to match water conditions, can be deadly.

At the *tailout* of a run, as the water thins, fly selection, smaller flies, and a more careful delicate presentation becomes increasingly important. It is here that all the stream's offerings are speeding by at or near the surface. A strike and hookup at the tail of a run should be anticipated, and you should prepare for it as it requires a more strategic plan to turn the fish before it is aided by the swift current and power of the upcoming riffle or following water.

Be observant at all times for *seams* in a run. A seam being the parallel line of water where two current lanes of different speeds meet. These can be caused by any number of conditions: the confluence of an inlet stream to the main water; a large boulder, rock or other obstruction; or at midstream, because of a convergence of currents, below a

Even the small ones are fun!

gravel bar. Fish will often hold in these *stations* of slower water conserving their energy while being able to watch and dart quickly in and out of the seam where the bugs are drifting. These seams appear as a discernible line between more swiftly moving current and slower water. A dry or wet-fly, offered as a natural, will bring good results more often than not. *Always work an obvious seam* or the *current tongues,* the glassy "slick" water between or below the confluence of different current speeds.

Pocket water is one of my favorites to stream-fish. Ideal pocket water is not found on every stream and is usually found only in streams with a fairly good gradient, where, during periods of heavy runoff, a series of rocks were deposited and, as the water rush subsided, were left to deflect the stream flow.

Pockets can be found on the side of a half-submerged log, a boulder, etc., or any area where an obstruction has diverted the current flow and created a small pool of quiet water. Classic pocket water is a rock garden visible *above* the stream surface that offers small pockets of still water on their down-stream side. Given the turbulence of the rushing water, pocket water offers a more forgiving atmosphere for a less careful approach, since the fish's sight window and external auditory factors are handicapped.

You must be prepared to fish this challenging water. Pocket water calls for fully dressed, high-floating flies (if dry-fly fishing), correct judgment of line length, and quick reflexes combined with accurate fly placement. Since you will be able to approach a little more closely, you should also shorten your leader (6–7½') to help minimize drag in the tricky, compound currents that are often associated with pocket water. The short-line cast and the minimum amount of leader/line on the water will maximize the abbreviated time the fly will hold in the pocket before being whisked away.

Working a fly upstream through each likely lie.▼

Start by surveying the most likely holding pockets and the best position to approach these from either downstream or sidestream, taking into account the drag factor. Next, false cast to layout the amount of line necessary to position your fly to land and drift into the "pocket." A fish is only going to have a second or two to see, make a value judgment, and strike your offering with little or no time for close inspection. Cast your fly upstream or to the edge of the water feeding the pocket. Lift your rod just enough to keep a minimum of line/leader on the water, without pulling or dragging the fly. Also, try bouncing the fly gently *onto* a rock, so as to have the fly hit the rock, then drop into the pocket water. A maddening second or so, a quick strike and a fish is either hooked or missed! *Rapid-fire casting...heart-stopping strikes...non-stop action!*

Rock gardens are submerged stretches of shallowish (2–4 feet) streambed that offer pockets, albeit completely underwater, of protection from stronger currents, and can hold fish in numbers. Observing the surface water action through polarized sunglasses can reveal the optimum areas over which to drift the proper dry or emerging insect pattern. *Cast upstream to where you expect the pickup*, letting your fly drift down into the fish's "window."

As the fish sees it:
A view from below

An important consideration in reading the water for likely lies, and for your presentation, is the factor of how a fish sees things. A fish's vision differs from ours in several ways. The placement of the eyes and evolutionary adaptation allows it to see objects from either eye independently or to use them together.

With trout, in particular, discrimination of shape and color are excellent and play an important role in their feeding behavior.

What a fish sees from its subsurface vantage point depends on the water type, depth, speed and clarity.

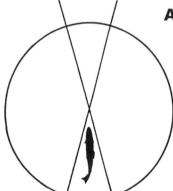

Blind Spot

Trout can see all but to their immediate rear.

Dry-flies, fished on riffled, aerated water or on fast, broken surface water, for instance, offer the fish a limited opportunity to closely examine likely food stuffs prior to making an instinctive move to intercept it, whereby sub-surface drifting nymphs and emerging insects are often easy prey.

The fish's view from beneath the water to the surface is affected by the refraction of light, and the angle and bend of these light rays as they enter the water. Looking from below the water to the surface, most of what a fish sees is a mirrored reflection of the bottom, with the exception of the telltale revealing dent or dimple of a fallen insect on the underneath side of the water's surface film.

The exception to this view is the conical "window," emanating from the fish's eye to the surface. This cone extends to the front and around both sides, but not to the immediate rear. To a fish eyeing an object on the surface, this field of view is sharpest at its center, with objects becoming less clearly defined as they move towards the edges of this window.

In shallow, choppy water trout have a narrower cone of vision. You can, therefore, come closer to the fish, but your fly must be presented directly to them.

COURTESY OF 3M/SCIENTIFIC ANGLERS

Depending on the depth a trout is holding or cruising, the size of this cone-shaped window will vary; the more shallow the depth, the smaller the window.

What does all this mean to the fly-fisher? To understand what a fish sees better enables us to select the best method of fishing, correct placement and type of fly. A light dry-fly, for instance, will sit on the surface film and will only be visible as it enters this cone of vision, while a larger or slightly sunken fly may protrude through the water's surface tension, offering a more visible target in certain water conditions. Fly selection and placement then become important considerations if we're going to maximize our chances of a hookup.

Knowing or suspecting where there are holding fish and an approximation of the water's depth is a determining factor for fly placement, as you want the fish to see and react to your fly before either leader or line disturb it. A fly, presented ahead and to one side of a fish, will drift naturally into its field of view. Fish lying in shallow water, however, will require a more accurate fly placement if it is to pass into the fish's greatly reduced viewing area.

These windows obviously move with the fish. In the case of lake fishing to rising fish (that is, fish moving beneath the surface, picking bugs off the surface), the objective of the angler is to observe the direction and speed of the cruising fish and *to anticipate* where to place the fly so it appears in the fish's mobile field-of-view.

It's also important when stalking our wild and wary quarry to make a low and careful approach to likely areas, as a fish can see you coming at some distance depending on its depth, the direction of your approach and surface conditions. Avoid sudden movements and silhouetting yourself against the sky. Muted or subdued clothing, awareness of where your rod and your own shadow falls, minimizing reflections off your equipment, and use of available cover to break up your outline, are appropriate in most open, quiet water conditions.

The cone of vision moves with the fish.

Metamorphosis

As we know, all fish are opportunistic feeders and will ingest a variety of foodstuffs that make up their daily menu: leeches, worms, crustaceans, small mammals and most of all—*insects*. Without going into specific detail, it is important to know the basic life cycle of this most important part of a trout's eating pattern if we are to successfully select both the proper technique and fly for a given situation.

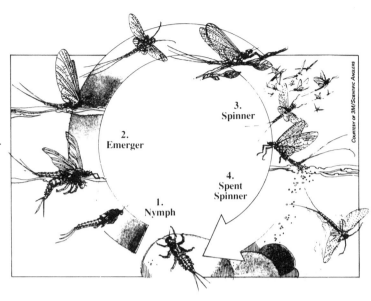

▲ *The mayfly's life cycle moves through the nymph, emerger, dun, spinner, and spent spinner stages.*

Broadly, these insects fall into two categories: those living on the land (terrestrials) and those that spend most of their life living in the water (aquatics). The former includes ants, crickets, 'hoppers, beetles, and the like. The aquatic variety most significantly are comprised of mayflies, stoneflies, caddisflies and midges. Although each of the four orders has distinct traits and patterns to their life-cycle, they share a commonality: they spend the greater part of their early life as nymphs or larvae clinging, crawling, swimming and living in and off the stream or river's bottom or its rocky debris. As this stage progresses, each in its own fashion, they move to the surface to enter the next phase of their life cycle.

Mayflies, for instance, live a year or so under water. As a mayfly nymph matures and swims its way to the surface, it will split its husk and the *dun* will sit on the surface momentarily, drying its wings prior to flight. During this stage of the "hatch" the dun is vulnerable both as it rises to the surface as an *emerger* and as it sits *on the surface* tension waiting for its wings to harden. A swirl at or near

Mayfly Adult

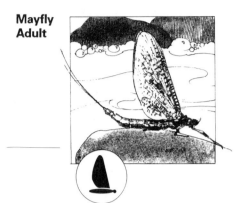

Stonefly Adult

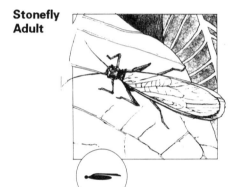

Caddisfly Adult

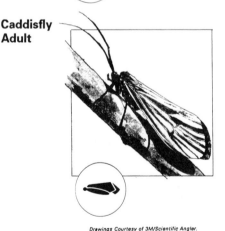

Drawings Courtesy of 3M/Scientific Angler.

These adult stoneflies and caddisflies are abundant in fast water.

the surface is a sign of a trout taking an emerger, while a slurp or bubble usually indicates a dun taken on the surface prior to flight. Once airborne, the dun is temporarily safe as it alights on the nearby vegetation, to rest until it alights again a few days later to lay its eggs on the water and subsequently die, as a so-called *spinner*. It is here that again nature offers it to the fish and where a tell-tale ring or perhaps a more overt head and tail rise can be observed as the trout slurps down the spent spinner.

The timing and exact metamorphosis of stoneflies, caddis and midges, while in some ways are similar, differ, among other things, in the manner in which they escape the water. That escape can be imitated by fishing a nymph pattern of the proper size, shape and coloring to duplicate the natural, either during its subaquatic stage or its release to the surface. Stoneflies, for instance, will migrate to shore or up onto rocks and surface logs to molt from their husks, fly off to mate, and then return to the water to lay their eggs. This is a vulnerable time for the stonefly nymph and prime time for trout to feed on them. The evidence of their "hatch" can be seen in the dried-out skeletal remains of their empty shells clinging to streamside rocks and vegetation.

The case-builders, or caddisflies, form cases within which they live, fabricated from either sand, twigs or tiny pebbles, cemented together by their secretions. Once transformed from larvae to the pupa stage, they too escape to the surface. Emerging caddis move very quickly to the surface and burst into flight.

These tent-winged insects drive trout crazy, as the fish splash and dash to head them off at the surface.

The point is to *read* the water. Rise forms not only indicate whether there is a "hatch" going on, but also at what stage and often what insect is coming off. Reading these signs gives you the best indication of whether you should be fishing a mayfly imitation, dry, an "emerger" pupa pattern fished just under the surface, or a freely drifted nymph to imitate one of these insects.

Once you decide to fish a dry or wet-fly, you'll have to make four basic decisions: *fly pattern, color, size* and *action* (if any). In wet-fly/streamer fishing, size and action (or lack of) is more important than color or pattern, although subtle differences may affect your success depending on water clarity and speed. Off-color water may call for a larger, brighter pattern to attract the fish's attention, while darker tones are less alarming to fish in clearer water. In dry-fly fishing, size and silhouette (pattern) followed by color are more critical, particularly if an obvious hatch is on, or in clearer and/or slower, thinner water where your presentation can be more easily observed. Read the water and make your fly selection based on the conditions present by matching what is most likely to be taken as food stuff before experimenting with a "searching" pattern.

I was up at Wyoming's Firehole River just recently and had a perplexing problem. Its thermal waters had cooled significantly from the previous few days to about 55°...I'm sure partly due to the air temperature dropping to 12° that evening and the 8 inches of new snow! I was fishing a size #16 Prince nymph and picking up some very feisty rainbows and nice brown trout in a flat, even run, but I kept seeing what looked like three or four dorsal fins just barely breaking the surface about forty feet below me. I thought that my eyes were playing tricks on me in the fading light. Why and what would these fish be doing feeding on drys when the landscape looked and felt like a scene from *The Night Before Christmas?*

I then looked down *onto* the water's surface and could see very tiny spent-wing spinners floating by me that were smaller than a size #28! Sure enough, these fish were slurping these down on a regular basis every few seconds. I made a quick change to the smallest dry-fly that I had, which was about a #20, but it seemed huge compared to the natural, and was "refused" on each cast. This type of selectivity develops when there's an abundance of one type of insect or another available and can happen during various stages of a "hatch."

Although this group of fish was locked into a pattern that I did not have with me to "match the hatch," observation of the activity and assessment of what was happening and what to use did offer a solution. Had I just one #28 spinner fly!

I did, however, eventually switch to a #20 soft-hackle fly that was happily accepted by several other nice size Browns that were not as selective, further down river.

Water Temperature

There are a number of factors contributing to being a successful fly-fisher. Besides knowing where to find their lies and types of water likely to present conditions that offer a favorable habitat, we need to consider the water's temperature.

Water temperature and the oxygen it can retain are interlinked. Colder water holds more oxygen; warmer water less. Likewise, the water temperature to a large degree dictates the timing of emerging insects and consequently the activity of various fish, particularly trout. So, there is good reason to carry a stream thermometer to determine not only the type of fishing you'll be doing but also the technique.

Early season fly-fishing in the mountainous region means cold, turbid, snow runoff. Water temperatures in the low 40's may mean a rich oxygen supply, but the colder temperature will necessitate placing your fly right on their nose, first so they see it and second because their slower metabolism will make them sluggish and slow to react. As the season progresses and the days become longer, the water temperature will rise, the hatches will increase, and the fish will become more active and turned on by the combination of an increased food supply and their more active metabolism.

If you arrive at streamside and check the water temperature and find it to be in the low 50's, and the day is clear and sunny, it's a good prospect that the best fishing is a few hours ahead. The sun's radiant heat will warm the shallows and thinner, slower waters first, making these the areas in which to initially concentrate your search for a prime lie, within the ideal temperature range for each species, as outlined earlier.

Conversely, as summer progresses and air temperatures continue to climb, fishing early and late in the day becomes necessary, for warmer water temperatures adversely affect a fish's metabolism due to the depletion of the water's oxygen-carrying ability. Temperatures of 58° may be the optimum for trout, but above the mid-60's they become stressed and will either move to more oxygenated water, if available, or slow down their metabolism and activity in order to survive. Smallmouth and largemouth bass and other so-called panfish, however, will find their ideal temperature in the high 60's to low 70's and are thusly called "warm water fish." By reading the water temperature, you'll glean important clues about insect activity and fish's behavior, and will more accurately predict where fish are holding.

So, what to do when your stream thermometer is telling you that the water is warming beyond the ideal temperature for your quarry? *Seek out cooler, more aerated water.* Fish the riffles and in the heads of pools that are fed by their freshly oxygenated flow. Seek deeper runs that offer cooler water, as well as the depths of pools that may be fed by cool, underground springs. Look for the inlet of feeder streams into the main water, that offer the influx of spring water or the last of the cooler mountain runoff. Fish the pocket water around whitewater and other areas below cascading, aerated water. Cast to where you expect to find fish because of the conditions present. If these areas don't pay off, then take a break mid-day and save your energy for the cooler, earlier evening, especially that last hour before dark when you'll get into some of the best action of a hot summer's day. Have your equipment checked and prepared with a fresh leader and fly, and be ready and on the water when the birds and bats come out to pick the bugs out of the air in mid-flight. Some of the biggest fish of the day and the most action can come in the warm, fading light of a summer's evening.

Some of the "day's" best fishing is during the last minutes of the fading light. ▼

You can't read a closed book, nor can you successfully fish a stretch of water without reading what it has to say. Reading the water takes in a myriad of factors from the fish's environment and subsequent behavior to your approach and technique. Careful observation, becoming adept at reading and analyzing what you see and what it means to you as a fly-fisher, will determine where, how and what fly to use and will determine your success rate. When you get to an area where you plan to fish, scout around for the most "fishy" looking water. *Look around.* See where the various lies are located. Look for *rise forms*, the tell-tale sign of feeding fish, as outlined in succeeding chapters. Is that a surface rise? If so, what is hatching? Is it being taken on the surface or just below? Look *at* the surface of the water. Are "bugs" floating by? Listen. Often you'll *hear* the splashy rise of a feeding fish in a direction other than that in which you are looking. Look *into* the water. (This is where polarized sunglasses help.) Is that a fish finning in the current? In flat, calm water lies may be more difficult to locate. Look for the fish themselves, finning in the current, or for their shadow on the bottom. Polarized sunglasses help in this regard. Was that "flash" the sides of a trout as it picked up a nymph? Thoroughly fish the water, timing your progress to match conditions. When the action is slow, cover more water. Conversely, when the action is fast, slow down and cover the water more thoroughly.

The water types, as noted, may be present in one or more forms in any given river. Water levels, temperature and time of day will all play a part and influence a fish's behavior—and consequently your success rate. Make mental and written notes for future reference. Keep a log (see Chapter Seven). A good lie will hold fish year-after-year. Conversely, vacant water, with its lack of contributory elements to the fish's benefit, will remain vacant season-after-season. Learn to know what's good and what isn't, and *you'll soon be an expert!*

Learn to read the water, for by being aware of the basic needs of fish and the various types of water in which they are found, you can concentrate your time on those areas that are most likely to contain the greatest number...and size of fish. Avoid any unproductive stretches and sections of water that contain few fish. Instead, systematically cover and work those areas that contain the environmental conditions necessary to support the best fish. This will add up to not only a higher number of hook-ups, but a number of *larger* fish—and greater enjoyment and satisfaction.

Read and listen to what the water has to tell you. You'll learn where to fish, what type of fly to use, the best size and color, where to make your cast for it to enter the target zone, and how to take the best fish the water has to offer!

A river raft can open up otherwise inaccessible streams of prime water ▼

Fishing The Fly 4

Let's get it WET

It's natural to start our entry into fly-fishing with the oldest, most traditional style. Wet-flies have been successfully fished for hundreds of years and, as such, probably account for the greatest number of landed fish. (Streamers, bucktails, and nymphs, though also subsurface flies, will be covered separately.) Classic wet-fly fishing represents not only the type of fly fished, but also the method in which it is fished. Wet-fly fishing, although often skipped over by newcomers to the sport, is again being rediscovered as it often works where other techniques fail. It is also the easiest method to learn and on which to build the fundamentals of reading current, drift, and line control while catching fish! Wet-flies were the workhorse of fathers and grandfathers because they not only imitate a wide variety of insects but their manipulation (or lack of) could bring a strike from otherwise uninterested fish. An added bonus is that you can fish wet-flies right from opening day of the fishing season, when waters are often higher and colder, and the absence of any hatching insects make dry-fly fishing much less productive.

Learning with wets has the additional advantage of being forgiven for an occasional lapse of line control and impartation of drag, until line control can be mastered. The double-taper line from your basic outfit also will serve you well in wet-fly fishing as its long, tapered forward section will allow your wet-flies to quickly sink, as intended, while its floating quality allows for easier pickup and line control.

▲ *Russian River Steelhead*

Wet-flies fall into two broad categories: those that imitate the natural (the duller, darker patterns) and those that attract or excite a fish into striking (the brighter flies tied with tinsel, or a white wing). Some fly patterns by virtue of their design and/or method of being fished trap a tiny air bubble or two within their hackle. The reflection of light from this silvery bubble is thought to simulate the flash off the sides of any number of small baitfish, as does the flash of a down-swept white wing or the bright wire and tinsel of some of the more gaudy fly patterns. Given the predatory nature of fish, the often obscured visibility and the necessity for a quick response to a quickly passing morsel, a trout will take this flash off the fly for the side of a baitfish and strike to intercept it, hooking itself in the process.

In any of our fishing techniques, be it dry-fly fishing, wet-fly fishing, etc., we need to assume that you've done your homework and selected water that is known to contain fish. Nothing builds confidence and accelerates learning speed like success. There is plenty of good water around, and advice from friends, the local paper's weekly fishing column, or a local fly shop can help point you in the right direction. Once on the water, stop and mentally review all that we discussed as to water types, lies, your approach, the method and type of fly that you use, and the like...*Okay, let's begin!*

The Wet-Fly

The classic wet-fly cast, in moving water, is an across-current or quartering "across and down" current cast. Observe the water, consider where there are fish holding, and think about where you want your fly(s) to end up. Begin with a short cast straight across stream or slightly upstream in deeper water. As you follow the drift of the fly downstream, hold the rod up so that there is a 90° angle from the rod tip to the line. This slight slack in the line will allow the fish to inhale the fly and to hook itself.

As the fly drifts downstream, impart action to the fly as it sinks with rhythmic twitches of the rod tip until the line is drawn taut on the downstream "swing," pulling the fly upwards. This is when you'll most often feel the strike. Frequently a trout will follow the fly across the current and strike as the fly lifts upwards, simulating the action of an emerging insect. This type of strike, on a taut line, is very perceptible and will hook the fish without any additional hook-setting by the angler. A great way to start! The across and downstream cast can be made as outlined with

The correct rod attitude will allow just enough slack in the line for the fish to inhale the fly.

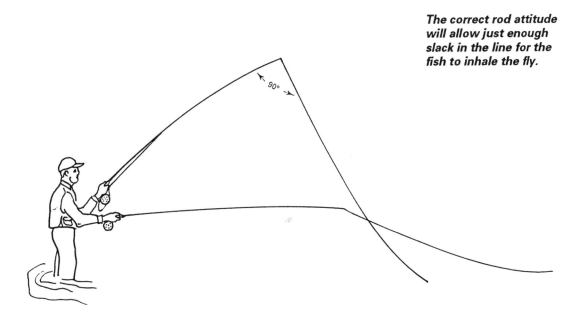

no manipulation of the rod, save for a mend (repositioning of the fly line), if necessary. Action can, however, be imparted to the fly by twitching of the rod tip and/or by taking in short strips of the line, thereby giving "life" to the fly as if it were a minnow or fry darting to safety.

You can control and vary the classic across and down approach by dead drifting the fly *naturally*. Cast across, as before, but this time *mend* as often as necessary through the drift to maintain a drag-free presentation and to *maintain the fly's speed at the same rate as the current*. Point the rod at the fly or follow the path of the line, where it enters the water, with the rod's tip. Alternately, you can dead-drift your fly, and maintain line control, by slowly *raising* the rod tip (and removing the slack) as the leader/fly approaches and passes in front of you, then *lowering* it as you complete the drift. You can also feed out additional line if you want to extend your drift into a target area.

As the fly completes its drift, let it hang in the current below you for a few seconds. This tantalizing action will often draw a strike. Strip in the line in short erratic pulls before recasting.

The next cast should extend the line out and across a few additional feet as you "fan" out and systematically cover all likely water. After a few casts, step downstream a couple of feet and begin again, covering new water in the same fashion. The completion of the cast and positioning of the fly, so that it rises to the surface ahead of a large boulder or other holding area, will likely bring a strike.

The *up and across* technique, is just that. A cast upstream allows the fly additional time to sink. An upstream

Wet-Fly Fishing – Up and Across Cast:

Extend back cast to "fan" and cover all productive water, mending, if necessary, to slow the drift. Move upstream and begin again. ▼

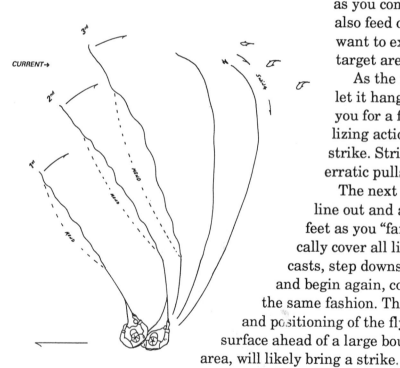

CURRENT→

cast, though necessary to sink your fly, sacrifices some "feel" for the take. After the cast, as the line drifts back towards you, strip in line *at the same speed as the current*, maintaining contact with you fly. Any visible or suspected change in your line action or feel should be reacted to with a strike to set the hook, much as you'll learn in nymphing. The up and across cast is also useful in sinking a wet-fly deep into the head of a pool where lunker fish like to hide and/or maintain their ideal temperature range within its cooler waters.

In the past, multiple flies were often tied onto the leader at varying intervals. The thought was to not only offer the fish a choice of pattern and to excite it with several selections, but knowingly or unknowingly, to fish these at varying depths. Multiple flies are not often fished nowadays, legal restrictions not withstanding; plus, casting more than two flies presents problems a novice doesn't need to be subjected to. If, later on, you would like to add a second fly, this can be done by either extending the stiffer leader strand at its blood-knot connection with the tippet or by tying a dropper loop onto the leader for the addition of the second fly. (See illustration in chapter on knots). In a two fly set-up the larger fly is positioned at the point and the smaller on the dropper. You may also choose to have one natural imitation and one attractor pattern to parlay your odds or different "natural" patterns, later switching both to the more successful of the two. The dropper strand's stiffer monofilament will help separate the two flies while casting, but you'll still need to slow your casting stroke and maintain a more open loop, as illustrated, to reduce the liability of the additional fly.

Whether you're fishing wets or drys, upstream, or up and across, continue to work your way in that direction. Conversely, if you have decided to use a downstream technique, then move *downstream* as you cover the water. This minimizes the chance of spooking fish *(RULE #2)* by

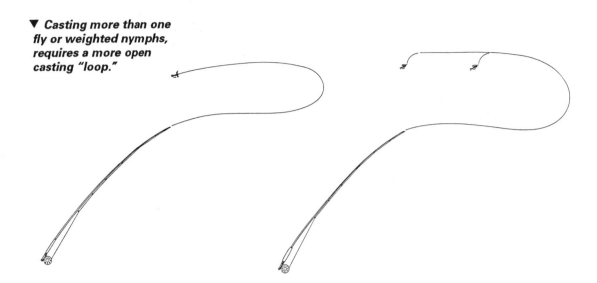

▼ *Casting more than one fly or weighted nymphs, requires a more open casting "loop."*

fishing water that you've already worked over or walked through.

In fast water, if you're not getting strikes and feel that your fly is not getting deep enough to reach the fish, then add a small amount of lead to the leader 10–12" ahead of the fly. Gradually add additional strips of lead or split shot to reach down to the fish's level. Remember to slow down your cast and maintain a more open loop to compensate for the additional weight.

Wet-fly fishing leaves a lot of latitude in technique. Don't let yourself get locked into one technique. Experiment. If the up and across method isn't working for you, try quartering your cast forty-five degrees across and down. Try working a fly or a pair of flies slowly across a pool, at various depths, tantalizingly working the line with your fingers, as you would in still-water fishing. A slack-line cast, casting so that the sinking fly rises on the tightening fly line just ahead of a holding lie (duplicating the action of a natural), will often bring a strike. Feed your fly downstream into the shade of overhanging brush or an undercut bank, where larger fish like to hang out during the bright light of mid-day. Try both a dead drift technique or manipulate the line to impart action and activate the fly, before you move downstream. You want your fly to sink as soon as it hits the water, therefore *don't make unnecessary false casts* as the pressure on the fly forces out the water thereby slowing its sink rate. Conversely, if there are surface disturbances caused by fish taking emergers just under the water's surface, yet the fish are not taking any naturals floating on top, then by all means duplicate the natural with a *slightly dampened* wet-fly (lightly dressed with floatant), floated *just under the surface*. Remember, short casts are easier to control and are easier to mend if your line develops a belly. Stay in control of your line and you'll stay in contact with your fly...*and the fish!*

Streamer Techniques

Streamers and Bucktails are flies tied to imitate baitfish, pure and simple. While a wet-fly can imitate a baitfish or an insect in varying stages of development being swept along in the current, or  emerging to the surface to take flight, streamers and bucktails imitate only baitfish. They are therefore sometimes considered more lures than proper flies.

Streamers are tied with a "feather wing," the wing being comprised of saddle, body or marabou feathers. The feather, particularly the marabou, will lie flat across the back of the fly when in the water under tension, then open up and "breath" and pulsate life-like when retrieved. The Bucktail's configuration is similar to that of the streamer but animal hair such as squirrel, bear, elk, moose, and the like are tied in as a "wing." The action of the current, and stop and start line manipulation causes the hair to flair out like the life-form it is tied to imitate.

Streamers and Bucktails are fished, in moving water, similar to the way the wet-fly is fished, that is up and across or quartering forty-five degrees down and across stream, and allowed to "swing" in the current or dead-drift.

As your fly drifts in the current, strip in your line with erratic pulls or pump the rod tip to give the fly life. Streamers and Bucktails are highly effective early in the season when the water is likely to be high and roily but the opportunistic nature of larger fish make their appeal as a "big meal" effective throughout the season. The cast is made slightly up and across, and the fly is allowed to sink and to *drift* downstream. Since predator fish strike baitfish broadside it is necessary to offer your fly in the same manner. The effectiveness of the dead-drift should include immediate and often frequent "mends." A gentle lifting of the rod tip and line and a deft flip of the wrist will throw the belly upstream (or down) and slow the fly's drift, allowing it to sink deeply and offer a broadside view to the fish. The mend, either upstream or down, prevents the Streamer/Bucktail from being pulled

Wet-Flies & Streamers

Top row:
Royal Coachman;
Leadwing Coachman;
Dark Cahill;
Partridge & Orange

Second Row:
Supervisor;
Muddler Minnow;
Mickey Finn ▼

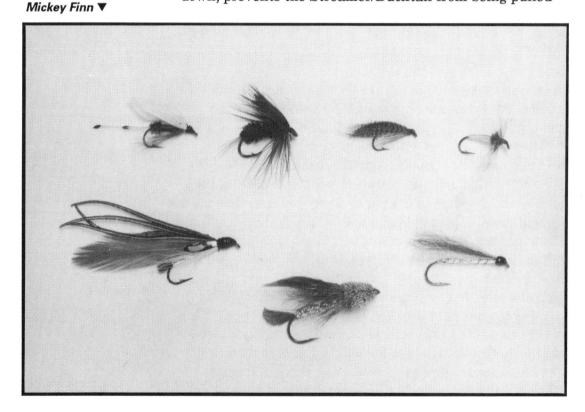

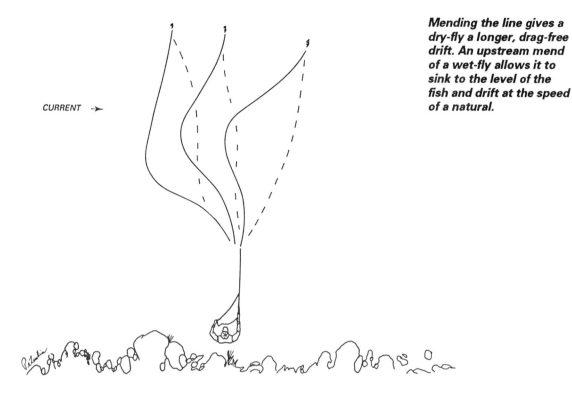

CURRENT →

Mending the line gives a dry-fly a longer, drag-free drift. An upstream mend of a wet-fly allows it to sink to the level of the fish and drift at the speed of a natural.

headlong downstream by the belly in the line. Cast, let the fly drift, mend, drift, twitch it, mend again, matching the fly's speed with the current's. As the fly begins its swing and as the line draws taut, throw an additional *downstream* mend to prolong its broadside view.

A strike can come at any time, but it is during the "swing" that it is more likely to excite a fish into a strike. Little or no effort is needed to set the hook, but since the take is usually hard, against the current, and larger fish can be expected, a stout leader is a wise choice.

Starting with fishing either wet-flies or streamers will get you on the water earlier in the season, condition your muscles and improve your casting technique, while at the same time it will put you in touch with fish on your first outing. Assemble a collection of flies, check the map, and *get yourself and your new fly rod to the water!*

The Dry-Fly

When we think of the sport of fly-fishing we are probably visualizing scenes of someone we've seen dry-fly fishing. The floating line and weightless fly make the tackle a pleasure to cast. It epitomizes the sport. To see a fish rise and move to take your well-cast fly is an exciting, satisfying thing and accounts for its huge popularity. Dry-fly fishing has its following of addicts because it is the most visual form of fly-fishing, holds a high level of anticipation, and therefore probably is the most fun! Dry-fly addicts will often forsake other methods of fishing even when conditions would warrant a higher success rate by another method, since it's estimated that fish take 85–90% of their food from below the surface (although, during a heavy insect hatch, this can switch in favor of the dry-fly fisherman!)

Fishing dry-flies generally requires an improved casting technique simply because most fish, feeding or lying near the surface, are more wary and a longer cast and better presentation are necessary to avoid spooking them. Being able to cast or shoot line 30 to 40 feet will, however, more than adequately put you in the dry-fly game.

You can successfully dry-fly fish whenever the water temperature is within the temperature range that each species is active (see temperature chart in Chapter 3), when there is obvious insect activity on or about the water's surface, or whenever it is apparent that fish are working in the water indicated by the appropriate rise forms. Water depth that is from knee to waist high is best, although deeper water is fine if evidence warrants it. In pools or still water, you can scan the water's surface and usually see if a fish is taking bugs on the surface by the telltale ring and bubble left behind by a trout sipping in a floating insect. In more broken water the surface rise can be seen and/or heard as a quick splash, sometimes exposing the head and tail, as the insect is plucked from the surface. This can sometimes be seen out of the corner of your eye, in a direction other than that in which you're fishing, in which case you'll want to wait for the next rise, to spot the fish and its lie.

Dry-fly fishing has three major elements: your *approach*, *presentation*, and the *fly* itself. Your approach is important first because you don't want to alarm the fish to your presence, and second because you want to set yourself up in a good position to be able to make an accurate, drag-free cast. Your presentation needs to deliver the fly to the water in the correct area to drift into view, without unduly alarming the fish, while acting as a natural would. Lastly, there is the fly itself. Viewing the fly from below gives the fish, in many circumstances, the opportunity to inspect it more carefully. The size, shape and color then become more critical.

Start with a selection of fly patterns suited to the water to be fished. Selection can be determined from recommendations of local resources, someone who has previously *(successfully)* fished the waters, by observation of the *size, shape* and *color* of emerging insects, or by using one of a number of basic, proven patterns that imitate a broad spectrum of insects. I've found that unless there is supporting information to the contrary, for most moving water, one of the flies shown on the following page will almost always draw a strike when *prospecting* an area. Additional "proven" patterns are highlighted in Chapter 8.

Size is determined by a number of factors, including the type of water to be fished. In fast, choppy water, you can start with a larger fly. It will be easier to follow in broken water, ride drier longer, is more visible to both you and the fish, and won't disturb it in the blur of the surface film. A size #10–12–14 is the mid-range for these flies. Conversely, in quieter, thinner waters, where you and the fish will have less difficulty spotting the fly, drop down several sizes, say to a #16–20. In either case, you're probably going

▲ Dry-flies

Top row: Light Cahill, Quill Gordon, Adams, Bucktail Caddis, Irresistible, Humpy

Bottom row: Terrestrials; Beetle, Dave's 'hopper, Ant

to change both pattern and size until you lock into the right combination. If you haven't prepared your dry-fly prior to your trip by a soak in one of the several brands of floatants, then you may want to apply a little spray or paste. This will assure a longer, higher float, imitating the natural it represents and make the fly easier to see.

When selecting your dry flies, at the point of purchase, look for those that are tied on thin wire, as heavy wire defeats the purpose, that is, to float. Check the fly's hackle. A poor fly, like some of the 6 for $1.99 hardware store specials, have soft skimpily wound, nonsymmetrical, soft hackle that will not support the fly upright on the water, thereby losing much of its effectiveness. Fly shops and catalog houses, however, have their reputation and repeat business to protect, and will carry well-proportioned, durable flies.

Watch Your Fly

The point of *seeing* the fly can't be overemphasized, the reason being that you'll be selecting a target area to drop your offering so as to have it drift, drag-free into the fish's sight window. In order to do this *you need to know where your fly is!* Has it landed where anticipated? Is it getting a good drift, acting as a natural would? Is there drag? When should I mend the line to avoid the drag and extend the float? Was that a rise to my bug or to a natural near it? And, of course, most importantly, when to react to a strike and set fast the hook!

There are several ways to know where your fly is located. For one, know how much line you're casting and where to *expect* it to land. A larger fly or one with upright wings will be easier to see if not inappropriate to conditions. A parachute or slack line cast can make it easier to spot your fly fluttering down onto the water. Learn to lock into your fly's silhouette as it will help you distinguish it from the background. If glare or reflection off the water is making it difficult to follow your fly's drift, moving your position by a couple of feet can help. A hat with a wide

Remember to keep watching your fly! ▼

▲ *Miller Creek grayling taken on a dry-fly.*

brim or visor and polarized sunglasses also help in this regard.

Prior to the start of your actual fishing, look around and decide the best water to dry-fly fish, taking into account the various lies present, your approach to the water, insect and surface activity, water conditions and the type of water you may prefer to fish. *Remember the basics* regardless of whether you're fishing dry-flies or wets, nymphs or otherwise. *Pick the specific area with the most potential for fish—don't fish over vacant water (RULE #1, again).* Also remember not to spook your quarry by thrashing around the very water you should be fishing. Exercise care in wading so you're not knocking rocks and stones together with your feet. Water conducts sound very well, and you don't want to unduly alarm the fish to your presence. Begin by casting a shorter line until you loosen up and get your casting technique back in tune to the way it was when you last practiced or fished. Take a few practice casts to check and see how your leader and fly are turning over. Make any necessary adjustments in your equipment to assure a good, drag-free drift. False cast only when you need to extend line or merely long enough to dry your fly. Avoid *lining* the fish, that is, having your fly line land on the water first, directly over where you suspect there is a fish or its prospective lie. *Reach cast*, if necessary. If you think there are trout holding to the side of an upstream boulder or other deflection, then make a few practice casts to estimate its distance and get a "feel" for the water, but do this off to the side or short of the exact area so as to leave the target area undisturbed until it comes time to make the critical cast, and the proper "presentation."

Dry-fly fishing is mostly done upstream as it minimizes the onset of drag. However, there are a number of factors relating to access that will determine whether you 'll fish straight upstream or at various angles *up-current* from your casting position. In moving water, you need to first survey the area for likely lies that will hold fish. Once determined, you then must decide on the best approach to reach and drift your fly to the fish, without either lining it with your fly line or disturbing it with your shadow or approach. Get yourself in a position from which to make an unencumbered cast, within the distance necessary. Work your way upstream. This allows you to come from behind fish facing upstream. Cast so that you place your fly so it drifts into the water at the rear of a rock or

Upstream and Upcurrent Dry-Fly Fishing. ▼

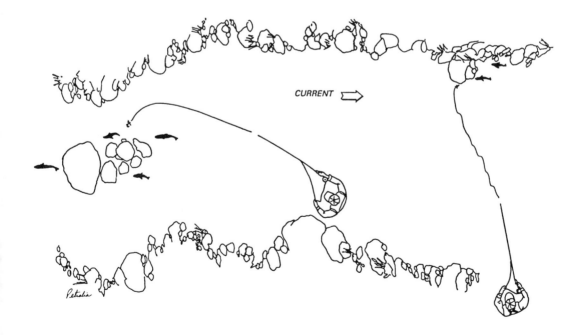

CURRENT ⟹

Petolia

boulder. The eddied water behind an obstruction will offer a fish protection from the current. After a few casts, extend your cast to cover the water to the side of the same obstruction. The friction will slow the water and sometimes harbor a fish. Gradually extend your cast further to allow the fly to drift in front of an obstruction, where a low-pressure area exists, offering relief from the current. Boils or upwellings of water indicate a boulder or other obstruction just beneath the surface. Be aware that this can be *prime water*. Cast to *each* likely pocket and seam, fanning out *from the near water* to the far, from each casting position. Work the *corner* of the tail-end of any pools, above the riffles, as you approach it. Cast to the water close to and above an undercut bank, or the outside of a bank or bend in the river. If the water's depth or other obstacles such as high glare makes an upstream cast and observation of your fly difficult, cast *up and across* stream into the same likely looking areas. *Position yourself* for each cast to a likely area to make the best possible presentation of your fly. Cast so that your fly lands above where you expect to find a fish, *so the fly will drift into the strike zone.* In either case, but especially in an upstream presentation, remember to control the slack by stripping in line as fast as necessary so you're able to set the hook on the strike! If your line is drifting downstream rapidly and you need to set the hook quickly, you can do so by pulling the line downward *and* raising the rod tip. Avoid making an inordinately long cast when you can maneuver yourself into position for a shorter one.

The term dry-fly fishing distinguishes it from fishing wets/nymphs and streamers. Your fly, however, may not be floating perfectly high and dry under all conditions. Choppy and/or fast currents can soak and partially sink a fly. This can be okay as long as your fly isn't "dragging" and acting unnaturally. Remember that fish are looking for food from below; a fly breaking through the water's surface tension can sometimes work to your advantage. In the various insects' life cycles, they're either emerging from, floating on, laying eggs and/or landing or falling onto the water. In some cases you will even benefit by fishing your dry-fly slightly *wet*, but remember *to keep watching it!* In fast, riffley water, make several casts to each likely spot to make sure the fish have a chance to see it and react to it.

If you don't get a strike where it's anticipated, your cast or presentation doesn't come off as planned, or you can't satisfactorily correct drag, *wait until your fly drifts past any potential holding or suspected feeding lies* before recasting. Don't "rip" the fly and line from the water you intend to recast to or you'll likely put the fish in the area *down*, that is, spook them enough to put them off their feed for awhile. Also, I've seen strangers and friends alike pick a good section of river containing fish and cast and recast to the same spot for an hour, beating the water to a froth. If there were fish there when they started, the only reason they would finally rise would be to tear off the fly and throw it at the fisherman to stop the overhead racket! If an area doesn't produce either because the fish aren't feeding or you think a few sloppy presentations have put them down (RULE #2), *then move on.* There's sure to be plenty of good water just a few dozen yards away. You can always "rest" the area and return to it later.

When prospecting a riffle or a run, *begin by casting to the near water first,* then progressively extend your casts to cover and "fan" the area. By doing this you'll avoid spooking any fish by casting over them. When you do hook-up with a fish, you also keep it from panicking the other fish in the water that you've yet to fish. Move up or downstream and again begin fishing the near water, and so on. Avoid the tendency to immediately cast to the far bank. Number one, it's probably too far to cast to *and* maintain good line control, and secondly, why should that bank's water be any better than the one you should have fished before you entered the water?

Systematically work the water by extending each cast to cover and "fan" productive water.

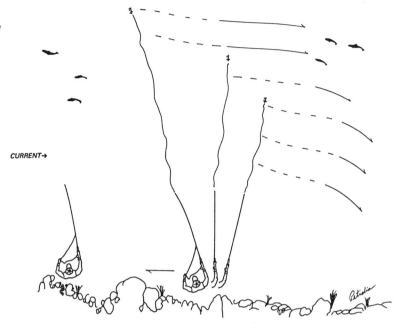

CURRENT→

Fish the *current tongues,* that is, the slick water and seams that separate faster water from the slower. Fish wait in the slower water conserving their energy and waiting to pounce on the food stuff (or your fly) these waters bring them. Look for a feeding lie, where the currents are concentrated, and let your fly drift through it. Place your fly upstream of a rock or boulder, there's likely to be a trout holding in the protection of the hydraulic cushion in front of it. Bounce a fly off that boulder and let it gently fall into the quiet pocket water below. Work your way upstream and cast into the still water behind each boulder, "picking the pockets" as you go. Cast a fly to the head of a pool or drift one down to the tailwater above a riffle. In late summer, try casting a grasshopper imitation over to a grassy bank and then twitch it until it plops into the water like the real thing. *Read the water.* Look for "fishy" areas. Think about your intended target area. Position yourself to reach it with a minimum amount of drag. Present your offering and be ready. Given the preparation, evaluation and presentation, you are going to get a strike...look for it...prepare for it...expect it...*React to it!*

If you miss a strike take solace in the fact that you've read the water correctly. Wait a minute and cast again—there is a good chance that you didn't alarm the fish or there is another being supported by the water conditions you've located. I'd rather miss a strike than not get a strike at all, at least that way I know there are fish present and I'll be better prepared for the next strike. *The action is part of the excitement!*

I'll tell you a little trick that I'll do if and when I can't get a rise and I want to confirm that fish are present but need to determine if it's the fish or my technique that is presenting a problem. This may sound a little unorthodox, but if I've spent a fishless half-hour or more over what I

This angler correctly "read" the productive cover of the water in the background...▼

consider "fishy" water and want to continue to fish with a dry-fly (sometimes against my better judgement), I'll try a little *game:* Is it my fly? My presentation? Should I switch to nymphs or streamers? Is it too cold or too hot for a dry-fly? Is it the time or the day? Well...let's find out...

I save my dry-flies whose hook has been accidentally snapped off, those that I've tied and am not quite happy with or those which have seen better days, and will *cut off the hook,* at the bend, leaving only the "fly" tied on the hook-shank. Given the above circumstance, I want to surface, if you will, the problem. I'll take one of these hookless phonies from my fly box and after situating myself in just the right position, drop it, untethered, to float *totally drag-free* downstream through similar, likely looking water to that I had been fishing. I'll watch it as it floats through a seam, around obstacles and into or past pockets, as long as I can follow it floating downstream. If nothing happens then I'm vindicated. But...if a fish hits it (and harmlessly spits it out) then I know that fish are not only present, but will rise to a *properly presented, totally drag-free fly* and that I need to clean up my act. I have also just located a fish to cast to! I don't do this often, but as I said, when frustration prevails, I do weaken.

When all else fails, experiment! No one has written the complete book on fish behavior. Sometimes, they strike out of a need to eat, sometimes out of instinct or perhaps curiosity, sometimes out of annoyance or to protect territorial claims.

There are times, for instance, when casting a dry-fly *down and across or downstream* is appropriate. If a rising fish cannot be approached from below or you cannot get into a satisfactory position to cast upstream, then cast and float your fly from above, allowing yourself enough additional distance from the lie or the fish not to spook it. A downstream cast allows the fish to see the fly before the leader and its drag-free float can fool a particularly wary trout.

CURRENT→

Store your experiences. A good fish taken from a lie will produce another for the same reason that lie supported the first. Try that spot, or one of similar character, the next trip. Anticipate where a fish will snatch a fly or where you saw the last rise *and cast above it*. Let the fly drift down to and into the fish's window. In any kind of current a fish will rise at an angle drifting downstream to strike a fly.

Experience will also show you that the gusto to which your fly is taken is not necessarily in direct proportion to the size of the fish (or the size of the fly). Small fish tend to strike hard and fast. Larger fish can sometimes be deceptively subtle in their take, therefore, judgement needs to be exercised as to not only the timing of the strike, but the amount of force used in setting the hook. Strike *quickly*, not hard, or you risk parting a tippet on a large, panicked fish. By the same token, I've had violent slashes at a large fly by some very small fish—smolts, fry—that I've actually back-casted right out of water, scarcely believing that their tiny jaws could mouth so large a fly! Conversely, I have taken fat, 18–20" fish on flies so small that I had a hard time tying them on my leader.

A trout will rise at an angle, down-current, to take a bug. Don't cast to where you last saw the take, but above it. ▲

As I mentioned earlier, if you're sure that you're doing everything right, in the right places and nothing is happening, then you have nothing to lose...experiment. If the water is "gin" clear and/or shallow and you're not getting any strikes or you can see a fish approach, then *refuse* your fly at the last instant, take corrective action. Make sure that your fly is not dragging. It may not be apparent to you but may be apparent to the fish. Change your position to compensate for possible unseen drag. Check your leader, is it straight? Is it *balanced* to turn over the fly, yet allows it to drift freely? Try changing to a smaller size fly or a duller, darker pattern. If a perfect drag-free drift doesn't work...try twitching your fly, like a caddis or stonefly fluttering on and off the water laying eggs. If a strong breeze is blowing, let your fly line/leader blow in the breeze, allowing your fly to "dap" on and off the water's surface, again imitating the action of an insect laying its eggs. A nice, dry, drag-free drift...but no hit...try letting your fly swing below you and "hang" in the current for a few seconds, *then* strip it in short quick strips. Find out for yourself what works and what doesn't, when all the classic, "proven" techniques fail.

Drag

Living wild in nature, be it as a land animal or wild fish, is a competitive survival situation, truly survival of the fittest. The aspects of shelter, comfort, food and instincts covered earlier assure the strongest of the breed will live and pass on their genetic code to further refine the species. In a fish's quest for food, it must judge by instinct, experience or otherwise, that which is good or bad. Have you ever visited an aquarium or watched other tanked fish? Sudden movement, vibration, light, etc., keeps the fish moving at a nervous pace. It sucks in a possible food source. If it's good, then it's kept; if not, it will be spit out quicker than the blink of an eye.

Float a dry-fly over or past a wild fish and all other

factors, such as color, size, shape, etc., being equal, a fly must act natural, *or at least not act unnatural.* Drag occurs because of variations in the current. Faster (or slower) water between you and your fly pulls on the fly line or leader, pulling the fly and causing it to create a tiny "V"-wake. This "wake" may be obvious or subtle enough not to be readily discernible to you at a distance, but it is very apparent below the surface. Whether the drag exhibits itself by the fly floating faster or slower than other objects in the same line of drift, it is making the fly *act unnatural* and will adversely affect your rate of success.

A fly dragging across a still lake or glassy portion of a run or pocket will rarely bring a fish to strike. (There are exceptions. Steelhead do occasionally like a riffle-hitched fly because of its action.) A fly that drags does not appear to act as a natural insect floating freely on the surface film laying eggs, emerging from its pupa stage or lying exhausted in its "spent" condition. So, if you are to present your fly as a natural, you need to eliminate drag for as long as possible, so as not to have a fish *refuse* your offering.

There are several ways to do this. Slack in your line can sometimes help by delaying the onset of the drag until after your fly has drifted over a fish or an expected lie, thus minimizing its negative effect. The *Snake* or "S" cast, outlined earlier, lays curves in your line when cast, to delay drag until the current draws away all the slack. The *bounce or stop-cast* can help. Here, you simply add a little extra power to a slightly higher forward cast and stop the rod suddenly as you complete the cast, to stop/bounce the line back towards you, thereby adding some slack. Shaking additional line from the rod's end guide (tiptop) can work, if the fly line is not directly over a fish *and* if you can maintain enough line control for the strike. All work in the right application.

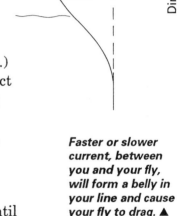

Direction of Current

Faster or slower current, between you and your fly, will form a belly in your line and cause your fly to drag. ▲

Line *mending,* however, is probably the method used most and with the greatest frequency for both dry and wet-flies in both the across and up-and-across stream cast. For, unless the water is of uniform flow, which it rarely is given the slower water on either side caused by friction, or in mid-stream by obstructions, your line will tend to form a belly. Generally, this belly is formed downstream by the pressure of the faster moving current on the middle of your line (if cast cross-stream). It can, however, even form as an upstream belly in certain water conditions. This "belly" will quickly pull on your fly causing *drag* and put down the fish. Mending the line *repositions* the belly upstream, delays the action of the current against the line, and extends the fly's drift.

To "mend a line" you need to make a quick flick of the wrist to flip the line (belly) back upstream (or down), thereby releasing the tension on the line and consequently

A quick, circular flick of the wrist, in the opposite direction of the current, flips the belly in the fly line back upstream, thereby slowing the fly and offering a more natural drift.

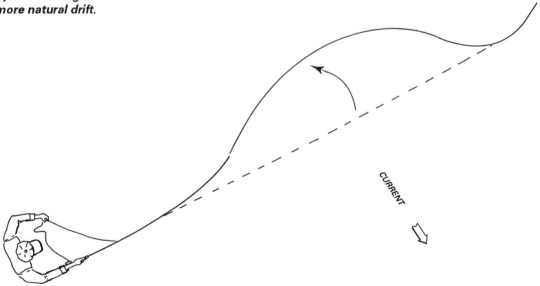

CURRENT

the drag on the fly. *A deft flip of rod tip will move only the line and not pull the fly,* gaining valuable seconds in your, now, drag-free drift. Practice with a shorter line until you feel comfortable, working up to greater lengths. As the belly redevelops, mend it again, if necessary, until the fly has completed its course.

Mending a wet-fly doesn't reduce drag, per se, as in a dry-fly presentation, but does slow down the subsurface drift, allows it to sink and gives additional time for a fish to review your more natural, drifting offering.

Drag can also be minimized by selecting the right position *prior* to casting. Casting upstream and off-setting the lay of the line via the *reach cast* technique is one alternative. Selecting a position down and cross-current to the water's flow, which will allow you to cast to your target area yet maintain line control, and eliminate a downstream belly

Casting upcurrent eliminates drag but remember not to "line" the fish! ▲

in the line, is another. Tricky cross-currents of varying speed can cause compound drag which can be frustrating, but again, sometimes a simple adjustment to your casting position either up, down or side-stream can better enable you to make a longer, drag-free presentation. In a tough spot try casting downstream with a snake cast, floating your fly to the head of those exposed boulders, gradually shaking some line from the rod tip to extend the float and getting your fly to the fish before the line.

One additional word on the subject of drag. In 99% of all dry-fly presentations, be the fly floating high and dry or half submerged, a drag-free presentation will be the most effective. You will, however, occasionally find that there will be a time when for various reasons, you will let your dry-fly come to the end of its drift and hang mindlessly in the current, wet, submerged and "dragging." Don't be surprised when, against all logic, you'll get a strike and a hookup when you *least expect it!*

This summer while up on one of Idaho's beautiful streams, I was fishing with a good friend who hadn't fly-fished in years. During the course of the few days we were fishing together, I gave him some pointers and advice as he brought his skill back up to par. Of course, I instructed him on the necessity for a drag-free presentation. On more than one occasion, as he dropped his guard momentarily, or as he adjusted his equipment mid-stream, he'd hook up with a rainbow as his fly dragged below him in the current. I was at a loss to satisfactorily explain why it happened although there are a number of theories: It may be because his well-dressed dry-fly, in just the right current flow, bounced on top of the water like an insect landing and laying eggs, or a fish followed his fly across the current and its tantalizing "action" as it moved in the current under the water was too good to resist, or his fly may simply be perceived as a struggling or injured baitfish and therefore an easy target. In any event, it does happen to all of us, sooner or later, so don't be overly surprised when it does. *It does not negate the "no-drag" rule.* All rules have exceptions and the 1% of the time when it happens is just such an exception. Take the hook-up for whatever reason and *enjoy the fight!*

Nymphing

What is nymphing? In its simplest form, it is fly-fishing using flies and techniques that imitate insects that live beneath the water's surface. In a majority of cases these insects spend the greater part of their life cycle as subaquatic life-forms, living in, on, under and around the rubble and plant life that comprise the streams and lakes' bottoms and banks. As noted earlier, most fish will regularly feed on these assorted life-forms. They will be the food of choice 80–90% of the time, as they are nearly always present. So, shouldn't it follow that you should employ the nymphing method of fly-fishing 80–90% of the time? Well, that's a legitimate question and can be best answered by the fact that, for one, there was little written about nymphing techniques until the last few years, and, to do so effectively, it takes on a different methodology, as well as level of persistence, to master this technique. It also takes a different mind set. Rewarding as nymph fishing can be, the less artful form of casting a weighted fly, lack of visual gratification of the take and most notably the subtleness of the strike, devotees have been slow to give up their dry-flies!

What it really boils down to is options: a well-rounded fly-fisher will employ the best techniques for the conditions present or, at least, have the option to elect a balance between the highest anticipated level of success with the highest level of enjoyment. After all, that's what it's all about. If it were strictly a number's game, it could start to resemble work…the antithesis of what fly-fishing is about! So, let's go about adding nymphing to our arsenal of tricks for a hookup.

Equipment for nymph fishing can be the same as for fishing drys, wets or streamers with some modification to the inherent parts of the system. Rods of 8½–9′ that are of moderate action work well. Many fly-rodders prefer the longer lengths of 9–9½′ to "reach out" with the rod itself, as a short line is often used, with little more than the leader extended beyond the rod tip. You could make an argument for leaning on the shorter side for its quick response time. Personally, I prefer a graphite 9½′ rod that can be best described as moderate to stiff in action. The lighter weight of the graphite is less fatiguing, as I reach and guide the fly through potential trout feeding areas. The graphite is more sensitive in detecting the subtle takes of the nymph and the moderately stiff action allows for quick, positive hook-setting, as well as more efficiently casting weighted flies. Also, the rod's action allows me to make a minimum number of false casts. I also find it is easier to make a *tuck* cast both into pockets and in up-stream presentations, than with a softer, slower rod. I lean towards longer rods, generally, and 9–9½′ is more comfort-able for me in directing my line and maintaining control. In nymph fishing, a natural drift is a dead drift and the longer length enables easier line mends and lifting of slack line off the water as a means to this end.

Mayfly Nymph

Fly lines for nymphing should be in the mid-range of 5–7 wgt. as often weight is required either as an integral part of the fly's construction or added to the leader to quickly sink the fly. Delicacy of presentation is rarely a problem unless fishing to trout feeding in quieter water on nymphs floating in or just under the water's surface film. Fly line color, however, plays a key role for the name of the game in fishing with a nymph, while mimicking the action of the natural, is *strike detection*. Lighter color lines, be they peach, light greens or other pastels are easier to see and, their action, as I'll explain, will signal the mouthing of your offering. Speciality fly lines are now being mar-keted that have a fluorescent tip, as well as leaders and add-on strike indicators that enhance your ability to detect a strike. For our purposes, floating weight-forward (WF) or double-taper (DT) lines should be used for moving water as they are less likely to cause unwanted drag and/or slack in the line that will be detrimental to your strike detection ability. Sink-tip and full-sinking lines are best applied to nymph fishing in lakes.

Leaders for a floating line should be long (9–12'), fine, and preferably knotless, thus, again contributing towards a quickly sinking, drag-free presentation, devoid of getting hung up on vegetation or other debris. A stiff butt section is recommended to help turnover these weighty flies. Conversely, you should use a very short (4–5') leader if you're using a sink-tip line, to keep the nymph at the proper depth. A longer leader can buoy a nymph so that it floats off the bottom as well as contribute to unwanted slack and difficult strike detection.

Okay, so much for the modification to your basic system. You should be able to use your fly rod, reel, and floating line and perhaps your leader from your basic outfit or to make slight adjustments or additions as needed. It now comes down to the *how* to's, *where* to's and *when* to's.

The basic rule of thumb is that you can fish nymphs virtually anytime there is no apparent activity to indicate fish feeding on insects floating *on top of* the water's surface. This is not to say that given your preference for fishing dry-flies or streamers that you couldn't stir something up and hook up with fish using any of these other methods, for you can, *but more often than not, fish will hit a nymph before a dry or a streamer.* It is what they do most of the time, for it is *available* most of the time. Taking nymphs requires less of the fish's energy, it's less subject to temperature changes necessary to bring on a hatch and there is a wide variety of clinging, crawling, burrowing creatures to choose from that are constantly being dislodged within a fish's environment.

Stonefly Nymph

Tailing

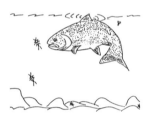

Bulging

Dimpling

There are sometimes visual cues to indicate trout actively pursuing nymphs. These are not always readily visible, and need to be interpreted correctly, but do provide important information. Categorically, these are classified as *rise forms,* that is, the tell-tale signs indicating the activity. Correct reading of these rise forms will dictate the proper set-up and presentation as well as greatly improve your success rate. These rise forms will be more or less apparent depending on water flow, size of fish, and most importantly, the depth at which the nymphs are being taken, but you must look carefully to see them.

In the shallowest water, fish can be seen *tailing,* that is grubbing the bottom, rooting out these immature life-forms from the bottom's rubble. At such times, the fish's tail can be seen exposed at the water's surface. Often, a trout must turn slightly on its side to take these bugs and may reveal its presence by a quick "flash" of its side. In slightly deeper water, water deeper than the fish is long, this tailing may be exhibited as a *swirl.*

Fish feeding close to the surface, depending on the depth they're feeding, can sometimes be seen *bulging* thereby exposing a portion of their back and/or their dorsal fin. Observation of the amount of disturbance will determine its depth, from a few inches to a foot and a half beneath the surface. *Splashy, noisy* rises usually indicate pursuit of quickly escaping insects, those that rise quickly from the bottom to break the surface and escape, such as caddisflies.

In the opposite extreme are the *dimples* or *rings* that radiate across the surface indicating a slow, deliberate, leisurely take. Fish cruising in still water or in pools can be seen taking these insects as they "hang" in the surface film, as should your imitation.

When approaching a stretch of water, *always look for these clues. Read the water!* Is there a hatch on, does it appear to have just started, or is it ending? Are the fish striking at the surface bugs or is that a bulge, a swirl, or other sign of fish feeding just *below* the surface, therefore, should I fish a wet or dry-fly?

Assuming that this is your initial entry into the sport, you'll have but one rod/reel to choose from, probably loaded with a floating line, with perhaps a spare spool in your pocket loaded with a sink-tip (F/S) line. The decision then is one of leader and fly selection and the correct fishing method, each dictated by your observations of the water at hand.

Often, no sign of activity is present but you know that fish are opportunistic feeders, therefore nymphing will provide your best shot at a fish. So, no visible surface activity in an area known to contain good numbers of fish? Let's drift a nymph...

▼ *A rainbow trout is netted...*

Nymph Selection

Fly selection will depend on the species you're fishing for and should duplicate those subaquatics that are native to the water, as these will be the most readily accepted. *Size* and *color* as well as *type* should be considered. These can be determined either by local advice or by a few minutes at streamside. A small seine available at fly shops or through mail order can be held in the water's course for a few minutes, straining any floating, drifting bugs, for observation. You can also walk the shallows for signs of caddis cases, look at the boulders and banks for shucked stonefly husks, or turn over rocks to get an insight into the type, color and approximate size of nymphs present and which to duplicate from your fly box: Sizes #4–#6–#8 flies to imitate stonefly nymphs right down to #20–#22 to duplicate midges.

▼ *Summer-run steelhead fun.*

Your selection of nymph patterns should lean toward suggestive or impressionistic patterns, comprised of soft-bodied forms that, when wet, will look alive. Soft-hackled flies and scruffy-bodied ones will suggest tails, gills and legs of nymphal insects as they float unwillingly along,  tumbling and turning with the current. Soft-hackled flies and those using marabou feathers can be effectively fished to pulsate and breathe, as will a natural, as it rises to the surface. Olive, tan, creams, light greens, greys and brown, as well as the darker tones, all have their time and place to be tried, depending again on what can be observed or is suggested for the area you're fishing.

Since nymphs will be fished on or near the bottom, except as noted earlier, weight becomes a factor. The faster and deeper the water the greater the need for your nymph to sink quickly. Some flies are tied with a bit of fuse lead beneath the fur and feather, or the nymph can be sunk by the addition of lead onto the leader. There are arguments on both sides as to the advantages of each. Proponents of the weighted fly feel that it gets to the bottom more quickly and is easier to control both in the cast and during the drift. The counter argument is that an unweighted fly will drift more freely, therefore, more naturally, simply by adding weight above it. Frankly, I've fished both and get fish on each. I tend to lean toward a lightly weighted nymph when I tie my flies, then add on a bit of lead as conditions warrant. These serve me well in all but the most still water, in which case I'll switch to a smaller size nymph. These I tie without any added weight or will simply fish a small no-hackle fly, wet. At times, when trout are taking either midges or emergers at or in the surface film, it is a grey area between a sunken dry-fly, a wet-fly or nymph anyway. Size, color, presentation and silhouette then become the criteria for success.

On the matter of sinking your fly, there are several ways to expedite this *without* the use of unnecessary supplemental weight, which can impede the fly's drift in shallow or slower water. Use a leader specifically designed for nymphing. These are designed to have high strength combined with a finer diameter and therefore will sink more quickly. Also, when you make your forward cast, just as the leader begins to straighten and the fly unfurls, *check the cast,* that is, *stop it abruptly.* This action will cause the weighted fly to recoil and tuck back under the leader and hit the water sharply. The nymph will then start to sink before the leader and line touch the water. As the *tuck cast* is completed and the fly is heading to the water, put the fly line under the rod hand's index finger and immediately strip in any excess slack. Elevate the rod as the fly drifts towards you, keeping in direct contact with the fly. Cast to pockets in front of and to the sides and rear of boulders, working the near water first. Cast, remove the slack, raise your rod tip. *Watch the junction of the fly line and leader for anything* that indicates a pick-up. A hesitation in the drift, a twitch, a pause, *anything unnatural* to the speed of the drift—*STRIKE!* Cast, retrieve, recast as you systematically work your way upstream, coming up behind the fish, and working the entire streambed.

If you do choose to add weight to the leader, one approach to sink the nymph and still have it act naturally and directly telegraph the strike, is to attach some weight to a dropper on a leader-extension as illustrated. In lieu of this you can tie a heavily weighted fly at either the "point" with a second fly tied in at the dropper, or vice versa.

Casting a weighted nymph requires an adjustment in your casting style, *as it is necessary to slow the timing of your forward cast. Allow that extra second or so for the back cast to be completed before beginning your forward cast,* giving time for the back cast to fully unfurl and progressively load your rod. Don't attempt fast, tight loops or you'll have wind knots in your leader that will astound you. The more weight added to your leader, the more you'll find that the "cast" begins to resemble a lob instead of a true cast. This tends to dissuade some people from the

two nymph set up   **dropper weight**   **lead on leader**

start. *Adjust to it*. Casts will be short, with a minimum of
false casts. Pick your target and direct your fly to it. Unnecessary false casts will only cause problems and will
unduly dry out your fly. Remember, saturated nymphs
sink more quickly.

▲ *Methods to expedite
the sinking of your
nymph(s).*

There are several ways to *present* your nymph depending on water conditions and whether or not there is a sign
of feeding fish. Visually survey the water and decide the
best place to fish a nymph. Your presentation should put
your fly where you expect there to be fish based on their
basic need for security, comfort range and access to food.

The basic upstream cast made in slower, shallower
water, is similar to a dry-fly presentation, given the adjustment in the cast's timing. It is important, however, *to
immediately sink the fly and to maintain line control* by
removing any slack. (A tuck cast will recoil the nymph
enough to have it drop into the water quickly.) The line,
directly connected to the fly, controls its movement and
behavior. It is your link to the fly and that which indicates
a strike. Line control is necessary because you want the fly
to quickly sink to the bottom where the naturals are, but
more importantly, so you'll be able to *detect* the strike. A
strike can occur almost as soon as the fly hits the water
and any slack in your line will be detrimental to your
successful detection of it.

Line Control

Throughout our practice casting and as you read and reread the section on dry, wet, nymph fishing, etc., and of course as you fish, be cognizant of controlling and tending your line. Your line connects you to the fly. The line and its movement, and its control, directly affects the movement of the fly, be it natural or unnatural.

Without the proper line handling you'll develop unwanted slack, have difficulty quickly setting the hook, and may be fishing your fly at the wrong depth. Line control keeps you in *direct contact* with your fly, telegraphing the right tap-tap-tap of a nymph just ticking off the bottom, or the subtle pickup by a fish of your fly. Stay in control of your line, and consequently your fly, and you'll land fish others won't even know touched their fly!

Working a gold dredge's suction hose fifteen feet

A Montana Cutthroat trout cooperates for a quick photo. ▼

beneath the surface of a river in the Motherlode, my partner and I got to see a lot of fish. The trout apparently became accustomed to our presence and would actually be attracted by the food stuff that the dredging stirred up. I'd watch them hold almost stationary in the current, moving quickly to *intercept* something almost unseen drifting in the flow. They'd inhale it and expel it as quick as a shot if it was not considered edible. *This is why you need to closely watch for anything that telegraphs a change in the drift of your nymph, almost to the point where you react by a sub-conscious sixth sense.*

In deeper, longer runs, your leader will need to be adjusted/lengthened to account for the increased depth. Rather than casting directly upstream, where strike detection is extremely difficult, you'll want to cast up and across, positioned at a right angle to the current. Casting up and across gives the fly a chance to sink. This can be further aided by the addition of the proper amount of lead on the leader, relative to the water's depth and speed. Split-shot should be applied several inches above the fly. The removable-type with their tiny wings or ears are easiest to use and reuse, or you can use a moldable soft lead or one of the flat twist-on varieties. Add the lead to the leader, a bit at a time, until the fly is drifting and *just ticking occasionally off the bottom.* As you make your cast, up and across, let the fly sink, retrieving slack and raising the rod tip as the line passes in front of you. This action removes the slack *and* maintains contact with the fly. After the line passes in front of you, begin lowering the rod tip, adding back the slack and keeping the fly from being pulled off the bottom as it progresses downstream.

Concentrate...be sensitive to any subtle change in the drift. Any bump, twitch, erratic movement of your line/ leader...*STRIKE*...short and quick. Watch for a hesitation in the drift of your fly line, or if it begins to move *upstream*. This indicates that a fish has mouthed your nymph. You'll be in direct contact with the fly and you'll know if it's a

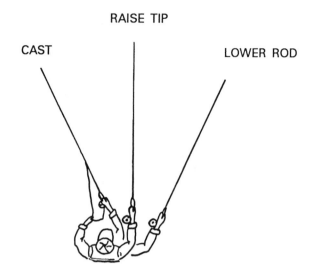

CAST   RAISE TIP   LOWER ROD

Raise the rod (thereby removing excess slack) as the line drifts in front of you. Then, lower the rod after the line passes to add back the slack, to keep the fly from prematurely being drawn up to the surface, and to extend the drift.

hang-up or a fish right away. It's better to *STRIKE* and not have a fish than to not *STRIKE* and miss one! If it's a false alarm, continue the drift.

As the fly reaches the end of its run and the line/leader tighten, it will cause the fly to raise up off the bottom. Just as in the down and·across method used in fishing wets, this can provoke a strike. A rising, escaping nymph sets off a fish's predatory instincts. Let the fly hang in the current.a second or two and retrieve it in short strips, then recast.

You can further improve upon the action of the nymph rising to the surface, at the end of the drift, by *planning* where you want this action to take place. The technique is called the "Leisenring lift" named after the Pennsylvania angler who perfected it. To maximize its effectiveness you need to locate a specific fish or a holding lie, e.g. in front of a mid-stream boulder. Make your cast far enough up-current so that the nymph has a chance to sink to or below the level that the trout is holding, as it approaches its lie. Your rod tip should be low to the water as the nymph dead-drifts downstream. It is at the point where the fly is just ahead of the suspected fish that you want to trigger its reactive nature to the "emerger." Smoothly raise the rod tip, thereby drawing the line taut and causing the fly to quickly rise toward the surface. If your drift is in line with the lie, the fly will emerge to the surface just ahead of the fish and *a strike is inevitable!*

Nymphing is short-line casting and you'll be fishing with barely more than your leader out of the rod tip, using the rod's length to work the line out in front of you and taking fish virtually at your feet. If, however, that ideal current tongue lies further out and a longer cast is called for, remember to maintain a balance between a freely drifted fly and contact with your fly.

A modified form of the reach cast can be used when faster current is between you and the water you want to fish. As the forward cast is made, *extend your arm and rod tip upstream*, thus keeping the line from prematurely dragging. Flip/mend the line upstream, to counteract the effect of the belly, should it form. This will give the fly time to sink and drift at a natural speed as you follow it. Mend again as needed until the drift is completed.

Another modification of the standard short-line cast, I call the *sling-shot* cast. This only works well with a moderately weighted leader, in the current, but involves virtually no cast at all to propel the line upstream.

We know that "load" in the rod powers the cast, so as your drift is completed and the leader/fly is hanging in the downstream current, the rod will be flexed and "loaded." A quick, deft lifting and redirecting of the rod tip upstream will pop the fly free from the water's tension, and will shoot the terminal rig back upcurrent for a new drift. It takes a little practice but is quick and easy.

In situations where fish can be seen dimpling on the surface or bulging just beneath it, try casting an *unweighted* nymph as you would a dry-fly, to have it sink to the proper depth as it drifts into their strike zone. Remember to wet the nymph first or apply a little mud or sinking compound to get it below the water's surface film quickly. Watch for the fish's take...a turn, a swirl or a flash...*set the hook!*

Strike Detection

In most nymph fishing situations, other than those noted near the surface, *strike detection* will be the biggest learning factor. We know that we need to get the fly to sink quickly by dead drifting it drag-free as a natural, ticking it on or near the bottom. Our success ratio depends on the presentation, line control *and,* most importantly, strike detection. To this end, various "aids" are available. Line manufacturers offer "nymph" lines with bright markings near the end of the fly line, leaders with bright orange butts in lieu of same and strike-detectors of various kinds made of foam, cork and yarn. Each of these greatly enhance our ability to detect those subtle strikes, since trout, for one, don't strike a nymph hard unless they expect to lose the emerger rising to the surface. More often than not they simply open their mouths and inhale, turning their heads and heading off the nymph as it drifts into their mouth, and exhaling the phonies almost instantly.

Strike-indicators go a long way in solving the problem of these subtle, all too often, missed opportunities. They can be invaluable in flat or low light, when overcast skies produce either a uniform or broken glare on the water, on rifflely/choppy water when watching your leader becomes difficult or impossible, or simply when it is easier to see the indicator than your leader. A strike *indicator* allows you to more easily focus on a single point so as to be able to judge any change in the character of your drift. Since often strikes are non-detectable because the nymph *doesn't move,* but simply *pauses* for an instant as it is inhaled, otherwise imperceptible "strikes" *can be seen* before being felt. A strike indicator allows quicker reaction time to strike back and, therefore, more hookups.

Strike indicators are available commercially or can be improvised from readily available materials.

Cork indicators are formed from dense cork that is cut into small, round spheres about the size of a pea, pierced through their centers and painted in various bright colors.

These can be made at home from either bass bug bodies, available from a fly-tier supply house, or fashioned from dense cork, which is cut and rounded with sandpaper, then pierced with a red-hot needle. In either the store-bought or handcrafted variety, the leader is then slipped through the core's hole at the appropriate location to match water depth, and a toothpick is wedged into the hole and broken off, to hold it fast to the leader. The nymph is then attached to the end of the leader/tippet.

Cork strike indicators should be large enough to remain afloat with the appropriate nymph, be it unweighted or weighted, but small enough to keep air-resistance to a minimum. Cork is buoyant enough to handle most weighted nymphs and is highly visible in deeper, choppy water.

A fat, Housatonic River Brown trout about to be turned loose... ▼

Cortland Line Company Co. offers a closed-cell foam strike indicator, with a sticky back, that is simply pinched on the leader. Both Cortland's products and the other generic foam types are available in highly visible fluorescent orange or red, packaged a dozen or so on a waxed sheet, like the old-fashioned penny candy. These are very economical, however once applied to the leader, they don't respond well to being repositioned, nor can they support a heavily weighted fly. They do however offer low wind resistance and are easy to apply and remove.

Cortland and some other manufacturers offer a package of one inch long sections of hollow (core removed) bright fluorescent fly line that is threaded over the leader butt. Given its small diameter, relative to the cork or foam, it is the easiest strike indicator to cast, blending as it does with the leader. Their small size and material makeup offer the least inherent buoyancy and are best used on smaller size flies or where minimum surface disturbance is necessary and easier detection is possible.

Yarn indicators are very versatile in that they're economical, come in an assortment of colors for both low and bright light, can be trimmed as needed to the appropriate size, float well and are adjustable (to match the water's depth) along the leader's length.

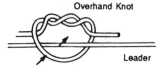

Overhand Knot

Leader

Yarn indicators, such as *Strike-Back®*, are packaged in fluorescent green and red in one convenient container and the yarn can be cut to the length necessary to meet water conditions. To use a yarn strike indicator, cut an inch or so of the yarn, lay it next to the leader, and tie a double or triple overhand knot to secure it to the leader. Trim the tuft of yarn to size and spray or apply a little paste floatant.

The yarn offers low wind-resistance but obviously should be formed no larger than necessary to be seen properly. As your familiarity and experience with a yarn indicator grows, you can progressively reduce its size.

The last alternative to the above indicator is a field expedient and probably the most interesting. Prior to tying on your nymph, thread a large, bushy, buoyant dry-fly, such as a Humpy, onto your leader. Make sure the dry-fly size is large enough both to see and to slide freely along the leader. After you cast, the dry-fly is used as a reference to signal changes in your nymph's drift. It can and will sometimes produce strikes of its own! Alternately you can tie on a large bushy dry-fly at the point (tippet end) and tie a nymph on a dropper, however, this fixes the indicator at a given distance from the fly.

Match your strike indicator to water conditions. If it's deeper, choppy water, use the appropriate indicator affixed at the proper location on the leader so that it will both float and remain visible. Position and readjust it so as to match water depth, keeping the nymph just bouncing off the bottom, as a dislodged natural would act.

Strike-indicators are cheap, useful and fun to use. *Try one. I think you'll like it!*

Little Mouths...Big Mouths

One of the best things about fly-fishing is that you can fish for any number of species virtually year-round. This means that fishing for so-called warm water fish may be one of the first places you'll start fishing, since it can usually be done closer to home. There is an abundance of low-lying running water and impoundments that contain a variety of panfish, as well as smallmouth and largemouth bass.

The general principle of casting either dry or surface flies has a common thread, but the technique, equipment and fly selection will vary somewhat by species. Smallmouth bass and largemouth bass, for instance, differ substantially in their habitat preferences. Smallmouth bass, in moving water, prefer water conditions similar to trout. Clean, free-flowing streams and rivers of moderate to fast flow, with rock and rubble strewn bottoms and temperature ranges (55°–70°) conducive to successful spawning are prime. Though smallmouth bass can be taken on small dry-flies during a heavy hatch, they're not as eager top-water feeders as their largemouth cousins. Smallmouth bass are scrappy fighters and their aggressive and prolific nature has pushed out trout in some waters where they've been introduced, legally or otherwise.

Tackle for bass fishing is dictated by the technique and flies necessary to attract them. In the case of smallmouths, fly rods that balance with No. 6–8 weight fly lines to cast bulky streamers or other quickly sinking weighted flies to imitate sculpin, minnows, small crustaceans and other crawlers, are ideal.

Largemouth bass are not as selective in their water preference as smallmouth bass and can tolerate warmer water (60–80°) with silty bottoms. They prefer lots of cover in the form of weeds, lily pads and assorted submerged *structure*. Much of the fun in fly-rodding for largemouths is seeing their explosive strike to the "fly," and this means casting a large, air-resistant bass bug, or other clipped deer hair mouse, frog or moth imitation. The most efficient means of casting these is with a rod of sufficient backbone and stiffness in the tip section to propel and turn over these larger (#4–3/0) flies. Eight to ten weight fly lines are the usual tackle for casting these bulky flies.

Whether you're fly-fishing for smallmouths or large-mouths, top-water or subsurface, your leader needs to balance with your outfit, contribute to turning over your fly and must be sturdy enough to hang on to these feisty fighters. This means a leader with a stiff butt section and a strong tippet. You'll need to experiment with different brands in the 6–12 pound test (0X–3X) to compromise between a leader flexible enough to maintain a natural drift and a stout connection to your fly. Strikes often come hard and you'll need to set the hook sharply in their tough mouths. Fortunately, largemouths are not particularly leader-shy and since you may have to "horse" them out of heavy cover, you'll need to buy an appropriate leader to fit your fishing.

Since flies are based on the bass' natural foodstuff, color, texture and action will influence fly selection. Yellows, blacks, and combinations of yellow and black, sometimes purple and blue or these colors in combination, will work best depending on the bass' mood at the time.

Fly-rodding for smallmouths on the Umpqua ▼

Bass "Popper"

Top-water flies used in fly-fishing for bass may be of the "popping" plug variety that are fabricated from either clipped and shaped deer hair, lightweight balsa wood, or the more streamline bullet shapes that "slide" just under the surface when retrieved. Other dry-flies are made with articulated parts or rubber legs to suggest life, while some wet-flies float *and* dive or use marabou or soft-hackle feathers to add realism. Largemouth bass like to attack their prey from heavy cover, therefore flies with monofilament snag or weed guards or upside-down riding keel hooks are useful to work a fly through the gauntlet of weeds and other obstructions.

If you plan to do a lot of bass fishing, you should invest in one of the specialty fly lines. A weight-forward, bass-bug taper floating line has a shorter exaggerated front taper that will help carry these flies. If your budget permits, a second sink-tip (F/S) line combined with a short (5–6') leader will allow you to *crawl* your wet-fly right along the rubble bottom like a crayfish or other invertebrate. A sink-tip line, combined with a buoyant deer-hair fly, will dive under water when retrieved, then float weakly to the surface between pulls, suggesting an injured (and vulnerable) prey. Also, by using the Duncan loop [knot] to attach your fly, you can maximize and enhance its action by allowing it to wiggle and swim freely. The loop will also add insurance on a hard strike by acting as a shock absorber, quickly tightening when a fish hits it but still protecting the tippet.

As with any fishing, begin with an overview of the water to seek out likely areas that will hold fish. Think about *cover*. Cover can come in a variety of forms: riffles offer concealment in shallow areas, undercut banks and ledges, shady areas under low-lying tree branches and bushes, brush piles, down or drowned trees, lily pads, weed beds all offer cover and security. Cover can also mean water of sufficient depth or submerged rubble or rock piles. *Read* the water. Look for likely holding water, particularly when it's adjacent to a nearby food source.

Largemouth bass like big meals and a life-size mouse or moth, cast close to a bank or weed bed, can entice an explosive strike! Bear in mind, though, that the same cover that they attack from they'll retreat to and fight from, trying every trick to foul your rig and break you off.

Consider your approach. *All* wild fish are wary, so don't put yourself at a disadvantage by a careless approach. In the spring you can usually find bass in the shallows on their spawning beds, and they'll aggressively attack almost anything they deem as a threat. Early and late in the day, or if the water temperature remains cool (in the 50°s), they'll cruise the shallows and weed beds for food. As the season progresses and the temperature warms, they'll seek the comfort of deeper, cooler water and the security of cover. Try casting a frog imitation into the open space between a lake's floating weed pads. Let it sit there perfectly motionless, *until all the rings subside.* Lower your rod tip, withdraw all the slack line and wait. After forty or fifty seconds, just "tweak" the frog to show life. If no strike comes, wait another twenty or thirty seconds and try it again. If there's a largemouth hiding in ambush, he'll spot your bug just as soon as it hits the water and attack it as soon as it shows signs of life. Their aggressive nature, the tension or fear of losing an escaping prey, will usually bring a "bucketmouth" to strike.

Keeping the rod tip low and even put the tip *into* the water, pointing at the fly. This allows you to manipulate the fly and move it the same distance as the amount of line that you retrieve, without the liability of additional slack. This is important when using either floating bugs or streamers because you want to control the fly's movement as you will not be able to set the hook hard enough and fast enough if there is any slack in the line. You may, in fact, want to strike with the rod *and* by simultaneously pulling down with the line hand to set the hook hard enough to penetrate.

Cast a streamer *close* to a bank or drop-off and count down…1001, 1002, 1003, and so on, then begin your retrieve. Largemouths, particularly in warmer water when their metabolism slows, prefer much slower retrieval speeds. Smallmouths generally prefer faster retrieval speeds and a moving target. Again count until you've reached the depth where they're holding "suspended" in the water column or until you can crawl your fly right along the rock-strewn bottom.

A buddy of mine and I were float tubing for smallmouths one day and doing quite well. At the end of the day we realized that while I caught more fish, he caught larger ones. We concluded that the longer, heavier leader I was using wasn't sinking as fast or as deep as his, so I was staying in the target zone of the small fish. His lighter, finer leader sunk more deeply and although he broke-off more often, the fish he landed were the larger ones holding closer to the bottom. Consider this as you let your fly sink during your countdown.

Bass are surprisingly strong, particularly river smallmouths which can use the current to their advantage. Even though neither smallmouths nor largemouths take much line, it is necessary to gain control of the situation as soon as one is hooked to prevent being fouled or having it throw your hook. As soon as the fish tires, take in line to land it and not overstress it. You can usually hold a bass with your thumb and index finger by its lower lip to subdue it as you remove the hook. Even though they are tough fish, bass should be released carefully to assure their survival by holding it a few seconds in the water until it regains its equilibrium, before turning it loose.

If you're fly-fishing from a boat for bass, or any other species for that matter, you'll find out soon enough that loose fly line will catch on *anything* that is loose in the boat. This will not only short circuit your cast but you can also bet it will foul you up just when you have a fish on! A large towel, old blanket or a piece of netting, weighted around its perimeter, covering all the deck hardware and irregularities, will make your casting less frustrating and avoid any problems during a hook-up.

However you choose to fish, be it from the bank, wading, or from a floating craft, follow the same general principles of applying your technique and fly selection to match the action and appearance of the natural that the species feed upon. Start out with the proven patterns outlined in the fly selection section, read the water, and *you're bound to catch fish!*

Lake Fishing

"Lakes" like moving water are called by various names depending on their location and size. Large man-made impoundments, reservoirs, farm ponds, small and large high mountain lakes all have their own character. As such, "lake" fishing offers another dimension and opportunity for fly-fishing.

Still-water can look like a blank piece of paper at a first glance, with no clue to what lies under it's watery surface. *The primary challenge with lake fishing is, therefore, finding where the fish are.* What you need to do is visualize and breakdown the surface area into smaller more read-able parts. Most lakes, except those sterilized by acid rain, or so high in altitude not to have the necessary oxygen to sustain life, are rich in aquatic vegetation and life-forms. By slowly viewing the lake's surrounding topography and notable features, you can usually ascertain some insight into its subsurface character. Man-made lakes and reser-voirs will have an inlet and generally an outlet, sometimes being fed by several creeks, streams, etc. Islands, remains of flooded trees, weedbeds, gravel shoals, protected coves, and backwater "fingers" define the likely areas to feed, protect, and shelter fish.

By far the richest areas, and the nursery for most still waters, are the weedbeds, both visible at shoreline and those you discover submerged within its interior. These weedbeds hold an abundance of insect life and oxygen. Sunlight feeds the aquatic vegetation, the vegetation, in turn, produces oxygen and protects and hides a wide assortment of "bugs," the latter attracting our quarry.

Reading a lake means locating the areas best fished early and late in the year as well as early and late in the day. For instance, the shallows, or so-called *littoral zone*, is best fished early in the morning. At this time the warmer shallows host the greatest insect activity, and given the thinness of the water, the least amount of security for feeding fish. As the morning grows, fish will move out of the sunlight into deeper, cooler water. Drop-offs, ledges, inlets, springs and generally deeper water offer a more comfortable and secure climate.

If you're accustomed to fishing moving water, a first trip

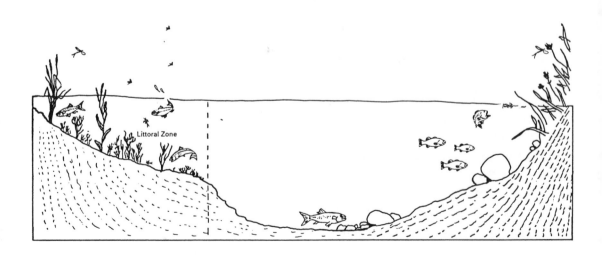

to a lake or other "still" water can be a mildly unnerving experience, unless you remember a few pointers.

A lake's submerged structure offers cover and security for fish. ▲

First of all, find out all you can about the particular water in question. If it's a large enough body of water, a map may be available either from a government agency, recreation department or local tackle shop. If so, an outline of its physical features showing access, depth, shoreline features, etc., will give you an overview (or underview) of its face. If it's a man-made impoundment, old features such as the original streambed (now submerged), dropoffs, etc., may also be marked. On smaller lakes, a little exploring from a high vantage point can help point out its key features and most productive areas. Also, when viewing the water, break it down into sections. Look at the whole, dividing it into those areas that are not only the most productive, but those that are most suitable to fly-fishing and access to the water. If you don't plan to fish from shore but plan to wade, a gradual sloping shoreline versus steep banks is what you'll be looking for. If, on the other hand, you have a canoe, small boat, pram, or float tube, you'll need to find some place suitable to launch. Any kind of floating craft will extend the range of water you can cover and also give you the opportunity to *troll* your fly.

In moving water, the food comes to the fish, while in still water the fish generally come to the food. But in order to fully profit from this axiom, we have to consider the nature of fish.

Fish, as we know are cold-blooded creatures and as such need to stay in a certain temperature range. Within the safe limits of that range, their metabolism will determine how active they'll be. Depending on the depth of a lake, water can stratify into temperature zones, according to the water's temperature and its density. The topmost area of a still body of water, or shallows, can even freeze. Unless it is an extremely shallow lake and/or a long, hard freeze, the fish will move within these stratified layers to their ideal comfort zone. As the season renews itself in the spring and summer, and as the sun rises higher in the sky, combined with longer, hotter days, these lake "zones" will change. This change of the thermoclines or temperature layers caused by the mixing of the warming water is what is called the "turn-over" of a lake. This change can happen in a matter of a few days or a week or more depending on temperature and the interaction of wind to accelerate the mixing of water. This turnover can be the signal for great fishing as the shallow water warms and fish return from the depths. Conversely, as summer progresses, individual fish species will descend again to the depths to find their ideal temperature range. Bearing this in mind *we have to fish our flies at the depth of the fish.*

Which Fly Line?

Floating lines are used primarily when there is surface activity, for fishing flies in the upper surface film or in the shallows. Conversely, sinking lines, be they full sinking lines or the sink-tip variety, offer the versatility to sink and keep your fly at the depth of holding fish. These sinking lines are available in different sinking speeds and depths. Scientific Angler's Wet Cel I, for instance, is ideal for fishing over weedbeds in three to five feet of water, while the Wet Cel II Hi-Speed Hi-D will carry your fly close to forty feet deep. The same specifications of sink-rate and depth are also available in shooting-taper lines and in sink-tip models. These weight-forward lines are great for casting longer distances when presentation is not as critical and the construction of the sink-tip offers the capability of sinking just the forward ten feet of line, making line control and withdrawal of the line from the water easier for recasting.

Still-water fishing for trout generally means fishing wet, unless there is an obvious hatch on. If there are obvious rises, bulges, swirls, etc., then by all means cast to them. A surface fly, however, needs to match those insects present on or breaking through the surface. Bear in mind

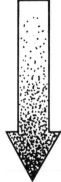

SLOWEST

FASTEST

Sink Rates:	Lines:	Line Weights:								
		5	6	7	8	9	10	11	12	13
1.25-1.75 ips	Wet Cel® Intermediate	•	•	•	•	•	•	•	•	•
1.50-2.50 ips	Wet Cel® Uniform Sink I	•	•	•	•	•	•			
	Wet Cel® I	•	•	•	•	•	•			
1.75-3.00 ips	Wet Cel® Uniform Sink II	•	•	•	•	•				
	Wet Cel® II (WF)	•	•	•	•	•	•	•	•	•
2.50-4.25 ips	Wet Cel® Uniform Sink III		•	•	•	•	•			
	Wet Cel® III (Hi-D®)			•	•	•	•	•		
3.75-6.25 ips	Wet Cel® Uniform Sink IV		•	•	•	•	•			
	Wet Cel® IV (Hi-Speed Hi-D®)	•	•	•	•	•	•	•	•	
4.50-6.00 ips	Wet Cel® V Uniform Sink			•	•	•	•			

SIX SINK RATE OPTIONS

3M Chart	
Wet Cel Intermediate	0' – 2'
Wet Cel I	3' – 5'
Wet Cel II	5' –10'
Wet Cel Hi-D	10' – 20'
Wet Cel Hi-speed	20' – 30'

also that a cruising fish will need to distinguish your fly from the twigs, weeds, and other flotsam floating on the surface. Therefore, a *slight* twitch can show life and sometimes draw a strike that a totally still fly may not. A high floating Humpy, an Irresistible, terrestrials and the like, in appropriate sizes, can be extremely effective at times. Gin clear, still mountain lakes, however, may require a more sleight, and longer, finer leader (12–15') and tiny #18–28 flies.

If there is a hatch beginning, fishing a floating line with an emerger pattern or nymph just under the surface film can be deadly. Dress your leader to within a few inches of the fly with floatant so that the fly just breaks through and hangs in the surface film. Match the size, style and color of the hatch as closely as possible, since fish can quickly become quite selective and still-water fish can easily scrutinize your offering. If possible, fish a hatch early before there is too much food available. Determine if the rises you see are fish feeding on emerging insects, or those on the surface. A "hatch" will progress from the emerger stage with fish boiling and slashing insects as they rise to the surface, then, as the bulk of the hatch has emerged, fish will start picking the flying bugs from the surface as they try to dry their wings and/or shuck their shellcases. Later these flies again become prey as they land in the water to lay their eggs and, finally, as they drop to the surface, their life cycle complete, in a "spinner" fall. *Read the rise* to determine if the fish are feeding *on* or *below* the surface and to determine the direction the fish are cruising. *Anticipate* its direction and *cast ahead* of the fish.

I had an opportunity a few years back to be sitting about a hundred feet above a large, clear lake in upstate New York at dusk. From my bird's-eye view, I could see a trout cruising along, leisurely picking bugs off the water. Each rise would be spaced ten or twelve feet apart. It would cruise for forty or fifty feet in a, more or less, straight line then turn a few degrees and continue. There was a pattern that offered a fair degree of predictability. Even if I could not see the fish as clearly as I could, the *dimple* on the water and the rings that radiated from it betrayed its position and pointed out the direction that the fish was cruising.

Keeping in mind the temperature zones, depending on season and time of the day, determine where best to locate fish

Observe the direction and frequency of the rise and cast ahead of it. ▼

▲Lake Flies

Top row:
Zonker; Matuka

Second row:
Teeny Nymph;
Damsel Fly

Bottom Row:
Wooly Worm;
Wooly Bugger

since fish don't have feeding lies as in moving water but will move around and feed in *cruising lanes* looking for food. Weed-beds, ledges, drop-offs, submerged logs, off rocky points all are attractive to fish for all the reasons stated earlier. Combine a weedbed or other shelter close to deeper water and fish will regularly come and go to feed into these areas. Locate the migration lanes in and out of these regions and fish them. Fish the shallows early in the morning and at dusk, when they are likely to offer the security to hold fish. Fish submerged weedbeds and submerged logs adjoining deep water. Look for areas of brighter green foliage along a lake's perimeter indicating a possible inlet of a cold water spring, a vital area in warm summer weather. Be aware of prevailing breezes that blow and collect drifting and blown insects, attracting fish to a lake's leeward shore. A snaggy area holds big fish because baitfish are attracted to it. Fish these areas with hooks tied with a weed-guard or those tied to swim up-side down, that is, hook-up, the so-called keel fly.

Match your line and fly to match the water depth. An easy system is to cast a sinking or sink-tip line and after the fly lands on the water, count: 1001, 1002, 1003, and so on. Each count being about a second. At a given count, say five seconds, begin your retrieve. Try this a few times at five seconds, then increase your count by a second or two, this way when you do get a strike, you'll know at what depth to reposition your fly, because that is where the comfort zone is and where the fish are holding. The fly line's sink-rate is printed on the fly line's box as a reference.

When fishing any still water, keep your rod tip low or even *in* the water. You will have much more precise movement of your fly, as you activate it during retrieval, if the rod tip is low and pointed toward it. You also can better monitor the rate of your fly's movement and maintain better line control by minimizing any slack by doing this. Any slack in your line is detrimental to both strike detection and accurate manipulation of your fly as you work your line in. Also, if possible, don't cast straight out but cast parallel to shoreline ledges and drop-offs, to more effectively fish the most fertile cover. When your fly is at the level that you anticipate there are fish, begin your retrieve. Try doing this at progressively deeper depths until you find fish. Also try very quick, short strips of line to entice a strike. Try crawling a Wooly Bugger or Matuka streamer right along the bottom, with a slow hand-twist retrieval of the fly line. Cast a Damsel fly nymph into the edge of a weedbed and retrieve it with a "strip and pause" action. Different conditions will warrant different retrieval speeds but start by *slowly* crawling your fly just off the bottom. Experiment until you hit the combination that works for your particular water.

Types of retrievers:
- short pulls—*slow / fast*
- long pulls—*slow / fast / erratic*
- pause—*pull*
- figure eight
- alternate—*experiment*

Best flies for still water:

Wets	*Emergers & Nymphs*	*Drys*
· Zonkers	· dragon fly patterns	· Midges
· Wooly Worms	· leech patterns	· Caddisflies
· Wooly Buggers	· damsel fly nymphs	· Mayflies
· soft-hackle flies	· attractor patterns	· Irresistible
	· streamers	· Humpy

Float Tubes

If you really want to explore new horizons as you expand your new hobby of fly-fishing, then you should look into the growing popularity of fishing from a float tube.

Float tubes or bellyboats as they're sometimes called, are manufactured from a shell of highly puncture-resistant nylon pack cloth that holds a truck size inner-tube. The better float tube units consist of a main compartment that holds the tube, an additional compartment in the rear that serves as both a backrest and as auxiliary flotation. To the float tube's shell are sewn an assortment of D-rings and handles to hold creels, landing net, etc.. The angler, wearing a pair of swim fins, sits within the tube on a saddle of reinforced nylon cloth and webbing and has at his or her disposal numerous zippered compartments engineered into the packcloth shell's design. These compartments hold everything from flies, spare reels, leaders, license, lunch, soft drinks, or anything else you can think of to take along on a day's float on a lake or pond.

The newest generation of float tubes have come a long way from the earlier designs. The nylon pack cloth is strong, rot-proof and extremely durable. Models vary by manufacturer but most have a second or even third air chamber in the rear, as well as a wedge or off-set design, to add additional buoyancy to the rear for safety and additional stability. With swim fins for propulsion, *a float tube opens up not only a whole lake but also access to its most productive areas.* Float tubes are light-weight, packable and, therefore, very transportable. They easily deflate and can be packed in your wader bag and taken on a plane,

A float tube provides portability and access to lakes, ponds and other water impoundments. ▼

or packed into a remote mountain lake—and *they don't cost much more than a fly reel!*

Fishing from a float tube is as easy as fishing from a floating arm chair, since your center of gravity is low enough to remain well-balanced and comfortable. Once in the water you can silently cruise offshore to explore productive submerged islands, areas of subaquatic growth and rising fish. From your floating platform you can fish lakes and ponds not fishable from shore because of limited or poor access do to weed growth surrounding its perimeter. By the same token, weeds and ledges can be successfully fished *along their length* as opposed to fishing them one-dimensionally, that is, at a right angle to these prime spots. You can also *troll* with a float tube, or combine a troll with a tantalizing twitch and strip retrieve. Couple

Easy chair comfort ▼

this with fishing closer to the water level without the leverage advantage of a fixed position and you'll really enjoy the challenge of a big fish tugging at your line!

Although not recommended by the manufacturer, you can even use these highly portable "bellyboats" to float a calm, slow-flowing river, gaining access to otherwise inaccessible areas. My friend Dale and I spent several days late this summer making 2–3 mile floats down a section of the Umpqua River, picking up bass and trout throughout its length. It would have been very interesting to see what would have happened if one of us had tied into a steelhead or salmon for which this river is famous!

As your enjoyment of fly-fishing develops, a canoe, pram, inflatable raft or float tube may be just the item to get into the water and into those fat, feisty fish that inhabit almost every body of water within an hour's drive from your house. Check it out; it's an option worth considering.

Where are they?

What to do when nothing works.

Okay, you have your casting down pat, a box full of beautifully tied flies, a new rod and reel, and assorted other goodies, but it's one of those days when you can't get a strike and can't get a hookup! What's wrong? Is it you or the fish?

Sooner or later it happens to all of us. What to do?......*STOP AND THINK*...start with the basics:

Is the water productive? Are you fishing over vacant water? *(Rule #1)* Why did you decide to fish at this place: a friend's recommendation or a referral from a fly shop? If so, it more than likely contains fish, but are you finding their lies?

Are you spooking the fish with your approach or your shadow? How about the environment? Is it clear, bright and sunny, making the fish skittish in thin water? *(Rule #2)* Are you taking advantage of the low-light conditions early and late in the day?

How about your fishing technique? More times than I'd like to admit, I've started fishing with a dry-fly because I like the anticipation of seeing the strike, when I knew another method would have landed more fish. *Fish the technique most appropriate to the conditions. (RULE #3)*

Has the weather changed dramatically? Wind—rain—a drop in temperature? A rapid change in barometric pressure can affect fish's behavior.

What is the water temperature? Too cold?...Too warm? Depending on the species either extreme will slow the activity and response/reaction time of your quarry. A good reason to carry a waterproof thermometer.

Back to your technique. What made you select the fly that you're using? Did you see a rise that suggested using an emerger and, if so, did you attempt to match the size and pattern to the natural? Check the stream's rocks. What size and type of nymphs do you see under them? How about that nymph that you're fishing? Is it getting to the bottom? Are you maintaining line control so that you'll feel a pickup when it happens? How about that dry-fly? Are you casting to the farthest bank, losing control of your drift and dragging your fly? *(RULE #2, again)*

How about your fly's hook? Are the fish "hitting short"? In other words, you're getting strikes but can't seem to stick 'em. Are you anticipating the strike and reacting too quickly, pulling the fly away before the fish has a chance to close its mouth on the fly? Check the fly...is there a hook left on it? Casting in and around rock and boulder-strewn banks can easily snap off a hook's point. Also, keep your fly's hook *sharp*. Rarely are store-bought hooks "sticky" enough and should be sharpened for surer, quicker penetration. Some flies in very small sizes (#20–28) don't have enough gap to allow efficient hooking. Carefully off-setting the hook slightly, with a small needlenose pliers, can enhance its performance.

What about your leader? Is it straight? Is it turning over properly, or is it landing in a heap around your fly?

Does it "balance" with the size of the fly you're using? (See chart in Chapter 1.) Check, and change it if necessary.

If after a review of the conditions as to where you're making your presentation, your technique, fly selection, etc., you come up with no obvious corrections that work...take a break! An hour or so taken to check out the water close by will not only reveal new areas to fish, *and* refresh you, but more than likely will be enough time to have conditions change enough, in your favor, to restart your effort.

Helpful Hints

- Fishing can be best early and late in the day when the sun is off the water, and in low-light conditions (dawn, dusk, overcast, cloudy, etc.).

- Don't wear bright clothes or jewelry that reflect light and can spook fish.

- Don't *line* your fish...*reach-cast* on upstream presentations.

- Cast to the *nearest* lie first and gradually extend and fan out your casts.

- Watch your shadow *and that of your rod* as you approach a likely area.

- Avoid wading if you can get into position without doing so.

- *Wade slowly* to avoid setting up ripples in the water, knocking together rocks and stirring up sediment.

- After a rain or downpour, try big flies and terrestrials as fish will be feeding on these drenched insects that have been knocked into the water.

- Stay low, move slow and *stalk* that big one!

Salt Water

Then there is saltwater fly-fishing.........

> *Once upon a time there was a young man who fly-fished and after years of pursuing game, small and large in rivers and lakes, he thought that he would explore the world of the ocean...for it too contained fish...so he tried fly-fishing in the salt. He discovered many things, among which was that he needed bigger rods and heavier line weights. These were necessary to cast larger, and/or heavier more wind-resistant flies, for longer distances for BIGGER and, almost always STRONGER, fish...What A Thrill!!!*

Beyond the mountains and lakes lies the sea and miles upon miles of shoreline and vast expanses of open water. Beneath its shimmering surface roam some of the biggest, strongest fish on earth. With few places to hide, these fish also have to be the fastest if they are to outrun the prey they are after—or soon become the prey themselves, if they aren't swift enough.

Saltwater fly-fishing has been around for years, but is just recently starting to really gain in popularity and receive the recognition that it deserves. Saltwater fly-fishing may mean the flats of the Florida Keys, Christmas

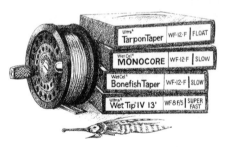

Island, Belize or other exotic places, or just down the road to your local beach or tidewater. By definition, we're talking about casting into the sea, be it bay, surf or backwater.

To do so, generally requires matched rods and line beginning at 7-weight on up to 12-weight. Such rods have the muscle to cast large, bulky, heavy, more wind-resistant flies the distance necessary to attract fish and also have the backbone necessary to handle their antics.

Ounce for ounce, pound for pound, saltwater fish are stronger than still water or river fish. They fight and they fight, jumping, diving, tail-walking, running, tugging, to and fro. *You'll love it!*

Saltwater fly-fishing requires an adjustment in your mind-set. Like the transition from stream fishing to lake fishing, you'll need to adapt your equipment and fishing technique to fly-fishing under a different set of conditions. Although you'll be switching to heavy rods, fly lines and flies, modern materials have substantially lessened the chore of casting these lines long distances. You do, however, need to be able to make longer casts to cover the maximum amount of water and to make a minimum number of false casts, as wind does become a factor in the open, unsheltered expanses of the saltwater arena. Learn and perfect the double-haul cast, as its increased line speed will cast further and enable you to shoot line and fly greater distances. Make your tackle work for you. The proper matched (balanced) outfit, in the correct line weight, becomes even more important when it is necessary to cast into the teeth of the wind. Modern line tapers, incorporating a shorter, more concentrated *belly* combined with a finer, stiffer, shooting line are some of the newer speciality lines that are now available to help maximize the performance potential of rod materials. The combination of the new generation of saltwater fly rod engineering and materials, revised casting technique, and availability of these speciality lines make the transition to the salt both pleasurable and exciting. These lines also offer you the ability to correctly position your fly *in the target zone,* both in the *horizontal* plane (distance from you to the fish) and in the *vertical* plane, that is depth. The correct line may be a weight-forward floater for the shallow flats, any

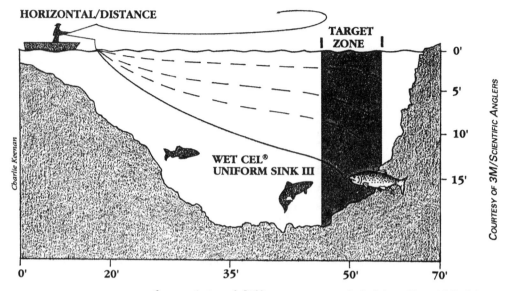

HORIZONTAL/DISTANCE

TARGET ZONE

WET CEL® UNIFORM SINK III

0' 5' 10' 15'

0' 20' 35' 50' 70'

Charlie Keenan

COURTESY OF 3M/SCIENTIFIC ANGLERS

Skilled presentation includes the ability to hit the Target Zone in the horizontal plane (accuracy) and vertical plane (depth). ▲

one of a variety of different rates of sinking line if fishing a shallow bay, or a section of lead-core or equivalent line such as 3M's Deepwater Express™ to get you down to the fish's eye-level.

Reels for salt water should be large enough to hold the appropriate line but also be able to hold additional back—ing line. One hundred plus yards of 20 pound and even 30 pound backing is necessary to slow and out-tire these long-running fish. Reels should also be anodized to protect them from the ravages of salt water and frequently rinsed and cleaned in fresh water to maintain their finish and keep the mechanics prepared for the strain of these stronger, harder fighting fish. A fully adjustable, smooth drag system and counter-balance on the reel handle are also welcome features to shop for in a reel that will be used for saltwater fishing.

When looking for a fly rod, think about the type of water and/or fishing that you plan to do. Don't buy a 12 weight rod when a 9 weight will be less fatiguing and will match the quarry that you're after. Conversely, if you've graduated to seeking out the biggest fish, then buy a rod with enough backbone to handle and lift that fish as it makes its escape to the depths of the ocean. Consider the added features of a larger stripping guide or a second stripping guide to facilitate longer casts, or the addition of a second grip or an extension fighting-butt to put muscle into the retrieval of your version of "jaws."

Match your leader to your line and flies. Ocean fish are often toothy fellows and either a heavy (60/70 lb. test) shock leader or wire leader may be necessary to help from being "cut off." Likewise consider your hooks. Stainless steel is commonplace to protect them from quickly rusting. Many saltwater fish have very tough mouths, so you'll need to thoroughly sharpen each hook to assure quick penetration and a sure hook-up. And, last but not least, these flies are heavy *(and sharp!)* so wear a hat and sunglasses...and *keep your back cast high!*

Yellow fin tuna from the Sea of Cortez. ▼

Marine fish are not quite as finicky as some of their freshwater cousins as the predatory reality of *eat or be eaten* takes on an even more dramatic role in salt water. The crystal clear water of the tropical "flats," however, will require you to call upon all the skills you've developed in carefully stalking and spotting fish.

What you cast to these fish is whatever the local species eats and what they eat is almost always either other fish or fish forms. Shellfish, baitfish, aquatic life of all forms as well as interesting, moving, exciting attractants can turn on everything from striped-bass, to tuna, to bonefish. A multitude of varieties of fish, whose names and appearance may not even be familiar, will come to a fly. That "fly" may be any number of streamers tied to represent a baitfish on the run, a crab, crayfish, shrimp or other invertebrate on its daily routine, or simply a popper that attracts a fish into attacking it.

Fishing the "salt" requires an elementary education in casting, the proper rod and line selection, a good reel and a selection of flies. Beyond that, specific areas to fish, the species available, and local conditions can all be gleamed from your friendly sporting goods store or fly shop. Armed with the basics, you can fish any water. All that is necessary to refine your talent is information on when, where and for what you'll be fishing.

Fishing the morning tide in an Alaskan estuary.▼

Fish On! 5

All too often in our pent-up excitement to "suit-up" and start fishing, we ignore a basic commonsense principle, that is, to *think* before we start wading or make our first cast. After several hours drive to our favorite fishing hole, be it a stream, pond or other parcel of water, an investment of a few minutes more to get the lay of the land is time well-spent. Too often you'll see anglers charging into water just where they should, instead, be dropping their fly. This is not only imprudent from a fishing point of view but also from a safety standpoint.

The Approach

Once you have your gear together and have donned the appropriate wading apparel, take a few minutes to look around the area you plan to fish. If it is a stream or river, note the volume of the flow and the type of obstacles you may encounter. Is there good pocket water upstream or down? If there is, *think about your approach*. Is there a dam upstream? Do they release water without warning? Is the entry to the water safe? How about exit? What kind of bottom can you expect? Should you be carrying a wading staff? Is there a hatch going on and, if so, do you have the *appropriate flies* with you or are they the "extras" that you just locked in your car? R-E-L-A-X...this is the fun part that you are about to partake!

An important overlooked point is that frightened fish can't be caught. Sometimes it's unavoidable but the fewer fish that you scare, the more you'll catch. Consider this in your approach and your movement into and in the water. Shadows, vibrations caused by sloppy wading, a "slam

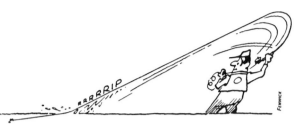

dunk" cast, *ripping* the line off the water, other panicked fish, or even sudden barometric pressure changes caused by unstable weather conditions can all put fish off "the bite." RULE #2—*don't scare the fish!*

Consider your approach to the water... is a stealthy approach warranted?...should your first cast be well back *away* from the bank rather than walking right into the water? Are you prepared for a strike on the first cast? It happens all too often and I, for one, still am trying to adjust to that very likely probability.

A few words on wading are in order. Once you've made the decision to enter the water, you need to consider several things from both a practical and a safety standpoint. If you're familiar with the water in question, you need to determine its depth at the point of entry and the type of bottom that you'll encounter. There is nothing worse than stepping off a bank and finding yourself going into water that's a lot deeper than you expected or sinking into a soft mud bottom. Once in the water, think about your approach to your casting position and move slowly toward it so you don't disturb the water and alarm the fish. If the current is swift, set and secure each foot before moving the next, shuffling as you go along, and progressing at an upstream angle to the current. Once the water exceeds the height of your crotch, it will exert a much greater pressure against your body and you should use good judgment if you decide to wade deeper than thigh-high. The close fit of neoprene waders offers a much narrower profile than canvas or even latex and are a definite advantage if you regularly wade deep, as I like to do. It is much easier to get into a tough spot than to get out of one, as turning around in fast water can be tricky.

Unless there is minimal current, in order to change direction *rotating upstream* is safer than turning downstream. A wading staff held on your downstream side will help stabilize you as you retrace your steps. Plant your feet, if possible, between mid-stream rocks. These usually offer a better "bite" than smooth, slick boulders. A little experience will prove this out.

If you should lose your balance and take a dunking, don't panic. Most slips just result in a shock of cold water and a little loss of pride, but you can usually quickly struggle to right yourself. If, however, you find yourself being swept downstream, some corrective action needs to be taken...*fast!* If you're properly outfitted with a safety belt snugly fastened around your waist, little water should enter your waders. Turn and point your feet downstream so you can see where you're heading and so you can use your feet to push off any rocks. Don't fight the current but use it to direct yourself downstream and into shallower water where you can regain your footing. Once back in control, depending on the season and temperature, change into some dry clothes as hypothermia (critical lowering of your body's core temperature) can be deadly serious.

Still water in either a lake or stream also requires a careful approach. Dark or neutral clothing and the absence of reflective jewelry or equipment is recommended, as is a quiet, careful approach into the water. Be aware that fish don't "hear" as we do. Although they have a form of hearing, they have what is called a "lateral" line, which is a highly refined system of nerves that runs the length of their body and allows them to "feel," as much as "hear," vibrations in the water. If you approach a lake or other still water at least make your first few casts well back from the bank. If you enter the water, move slowly to avoid setting up ripples that disclose your presence. Sloppy wading techniques, like kicking rocks and stirring up sediment, can ruin your fishing prospects for many yards around you. Look for, and be aware of, feeding lies, rises, surface activity and other opportunities for fish. Think about your approach to these. Get yourself into position to be able to cast into these areas without encountering cross-currents that will contribute to drag. Consider wading and fishing upstream so you'll approach trout from behind. Consider the time of day, how far downstream (or upstream) you'll wind-up and your return route.

This stretch of fast water offered up several good fish from the shelter of its irregular bottom. ▼

Years back, again during my prospecting days, I was working a section of my placer claim that was down a steep canyon. It was about an hour after sunset, and the light was dim as it fades quickly in the deeper canyons. I was camped with some friends at the top of the ridge. Just after dark, we were approached by a fellow in his forties, dressed in hip boots and fly rod. He looked exhausted and anxious. He proceeded to tell us that he was fishing with his dad and apparently neither was watching the fading light. They had fished too long, misjudged the time, became disoriented on the rocky streambed in the dark and couldn't find the foot path back up to the ridge line. The son, being younger and more agile, was able to muscle his way up the mountain slope. His dad, however, was out-of-juice and stuck literally between a rock and a hard place about three-quarters of the way up the loose shale hillside. I took rope and some climbing tackle and rappelled down to the older fellow, managed to get a rope to him and had the rest of our group pull us back up...creel of trout and all! As it turned out this old gent is a well-known angler and fly-rod builder and eventually built the graphite rod that I still use, the most often, to this day.

The point is, any of us can get into trouble and it's easier to *stay* out of it than to *get* out of it, so *plan ahead* and be aware of your surroundings.

So, you are on the water, your equipment is set up properly, you've made a quiet planned approach, your cast is perfect, the fly alights on the water and all you need now is a strike from a fish for which these waters are famous. So now what?...***Be Ready!***

Striking

Depending on whether you're fishing dry flies, wets, nymphs, streamers or other "bugs," you need to be prepared for the strike. Dry-fly fishing usually offers you the best visual cue. I say *usually* because not every strike is readily visible. Riffled water, a dampened fly, a subtle take, a momentary loss of the fly from view, etc., can interrupt your concentration and reaction time. You may have perfected your casting, purchased the best equipment and are on a great "fishy" stretch of water and STRIKE!...but are you prepared for what to do next? I'll offer you another short story:

My fiancée and I were up in Northern Californian's Rising River a few seasons back. I had converted her from a spin caster to a fly caster and had her outfitted in all my extra equipment...stocking foot waders, well-equipped vest, a wooden landing net, and a good rod and reel.

We entered the river at dusk and joined a half dozen other fly fishermen who were strung out along the river over a couple of hundred yards. The water was like glass, the air dead still. Quiet. *V-E-R-Y* quiet…you could hear the other fishermen talk in quiet tones up and down the river, the still summer night's air carried the sound. After five or ten minutes of unsuccessful casts, a fellow off to one side of her started a conversation, commenting on her equipment and asking how long she had been fly-fishing, a question I don't believe she ever answered. He then pointed out a rising fish and suggested that she cast to it, which she did…STRIKE!…the fish was on! I don't know who was more excited, Nancy or the fish, but the stillness of the night air was shattered. She then turned to me and in a desperate, muted scream exclaimed,"What do I do now??"

Up and down the river, it resounded like an echo…one fisherman after another repeating out loud for their own and each others' amusement, "What do I do now?" "What do I do now?" Finally, someone sarcastically yelled out the absurd, "cut the line!" thus thoroughly embarrassing Nancy and delighting the other "pros." The fault, however, was not hers but mine. I was so pleased with myself

Observing your fly tells you how it is behaving and alerts you to the strike!

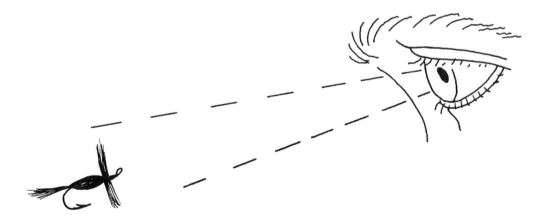

and her, having taught her *how* to cast, I had forgotten to teach her *how to fish!*

Too often beginning fly fishermen will attempt to master all the basics and omit the obvious, assuming that the fish will hook themselves. This does happen, usually when fishing wets downstream and with streamers. You'll feel the tug and the fish is hooked, an additional setting of the hook may not be necessary to secure it fast to the line. Conversely, when fishing nymphs, it is mandatory that you strike and set the hook, because as fast as you can say "trout," a fish will inhale and expel your nymph.

In dry-fly fishing, *look for the landing of your fly!* This is necessary not only to maintain a drag-free drift but also to set the hook. Small, dark flies on anything but still waters are always difficult to see, so anticipate where your fly will land and *visually lock onto it.* Point your rod toward it and remove any slack. Follow your fly with your rod tip. Mend your line to control the slack and drag. At the instant of the strike, quickly raise your rod to set the hook. Don't "rip its lips off," for if you strike too hard you'll part that delicate tippet and lose fly and fish. Instead, be ready for the strike and quickly raise the rod tip.

If you're fishing upstream in swift water, your fly line is going to be traveling back toward you very quickly. You will need to strip in slack line just as quickly to stay in control. Lifting the rod and simultaneously pulling down on the line, with your other hand, will take up the excess slack and set the hook. Conversely, if fishing nymphs across stream and maintaining control of your line, you'll be able to more easily stay in contact with your fly. Watch and follow your leader where it enters the water, or keep your eye on your strike-indicator, if you're using one. Any change in its drift or direction, relative to the current—a pause, hesitation, or visible sign of a fish taking your nymph—strike quickly and positively. If you're in direct contact with your fly, it will telegraph the "take," but you need to react quickly, almost instinctively, in order to set the hook.

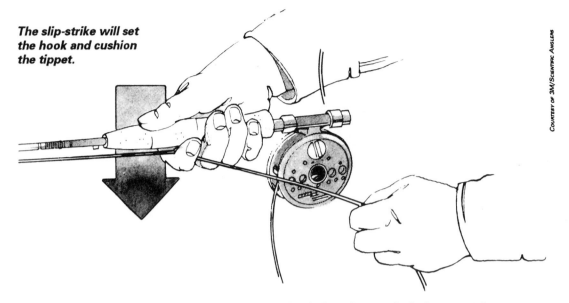

The slip-strike will set the hook and cushion the tippet.

A technique called the *slip strike* helps avoid an over-anxious strike. As you're working your fly and taking in the slack, keep the line trapped between the rod's grip and your index finger, as you retrieve the line. At the moment of the strike, when you raise the rod, the line trapped under your finger will "slip," cushioning the strike, but with enough resistance to set the hook. The technique forgives many an overreaction that would otherwise strain the tippet.

Playing

Playing the fish is a give-and-take affair (hopefully). If the fish is small, you can usually *line* it in, that is, strip in the line with your "line" hand until the amount of line outside the guide tip is roughly equal to the rod's length, thereby allowing you to raise the rod back vertically and draw the fish to you so that you can either net it or back-out the hook. I prefer, however, on all but the smallest fish, to play the fish from the reel. This was suggested to me early on by a friend as a practice in which to become proficient. As increased experience brought increased success and larger fish, his advice has paid off.

Playing the fish from the reel has a number of distinct advantages. Unless the fish is very small, rigidly drawing it in leaves the strong probability of the fish being able to make a sudden move and part a delicate tippet since there isn't sufficient cushioning effect. Also, loose coils of fly line around your feet, in either still or moving water, have their own inherent problems. A larger fish will need to be tired sufficiently before it can be landed and will need to be allowed to take some line. In order to best do this, the rod should be held high and at a 45–60° angle with the line connected to the fish kept loosely trapped between finger and grip. At the same time, *the loose line must be very quickly retrieved onto the reel under slight tension* so that it lies compactly on the spool. The fish can then be played against the combined action and cushioning effect

Nymphing a "run" on a swift northern Idaho river.▼

of the springiness of the rod, the friction of the guides, the stretch of the leader and the reel's drag. You can demonstrate this to yourself by tying the tippet to a rigid object and slowly pulling on it until it breaks, then try running the same tippet off the rod and reel and see how much more pressure it can withstand because of the rod's flex and the clutch effect of the drag. The few seconds between the hook-up and the reeling in of loose line can be tense, but there is usually a momentary gap between the fish's awareness that his potential snack had a hook in it and its initial run for freedom...but not always!

The only way to land a large fish successfully is to tire it sufficiently so you can take up enough line to net or release it. If you hook into a big one, and are not in danger of losing him into a downstream rapid in which you cannot

Extending the rod rearward allows it to buffer a fish's final surge.▼

follow, then allow it to run. Prematurely trying to check it when it's "green" and you run the risk of snapping the tippet.

You can regulate the pressure on a running fish in a number of ways: most reels have an adjustable mechanical drag that exerts a breaking action on the spool to vary the degree of resistance. Other reels have an exposed rim on the spool so that it can be fingered or "palmed" to slow down the fish. Also, you can use the angle of the rod and resistance of the line on the guides, with or without assistance from other means, to manage and tire a fish. A rod pointed at a running fish offers the least resistance, while a more acute angle will increase the pressure. Bear in mind, your tippet's breaking strength and act accordingly. The more the fish runs, jumps and fights the current, the quicker it'll tire. You will need to balance this with a pre-determination on whether or not you plan to keep the fish, for to tire it excessively is to handicap its chance for revival and ultimate survival.

The combined action of a strong fish and strong current puts quite a strain on tippet and knots. Also the longer you fight the fish the greater the possibility that the hook can enlarge the initial point of penetration and the hook can be thrown. You may need to let it take line when necessary, while maintaining control as it runs downstream, or conversely increase tension to turn it before it runs into snags and weeds that will break you off. In a stream situation, try where possible to keep the fish above you. This will force it to fight both you and the current, tiring it more quickly. This is generally easier while fishing drys because you'll often be fishing upstream or cross-stream. Turn your rod horizontal and parallel to the water for a few seconds so that the fish has to turn its head, first to one side, then to the other. Keep it fighting both the line, rod, and the current as you begin to retrieve line and work it into a calm stretch of water for landing. If the fish gets below you, heading downstream, you have to decide if you can turn it or follow it downstream, either by wading or following along the shore.

Allow no slack in your line as it makes it easier for a fish to turn its head and change the angle of hook which then can be more easily released. One exception to the no-slack rule would be if you're fighting a losing battle with a fish heading downstream toward a set of rapids through which you can't follow and in which you will certainly lose him. In such a desperate move, throwing enough extra slack in your line can sometimes have the fish resist the new direction of pull and head back upstream.

Several species of fish, from rainbow to steelhead and a variety of saltwater fish, will break water, jump and "tail-walk" in an attempt to throw the hook...*exciting stuff, but be prepared.* The greatly lessened resistance of the air, versus the water, combined with a sharp head shake can

Netting a nice one in mid-stream. ▼

Kulick River rainbow.

pop a delicate tippet. When this happens, *lower your rod* to give an instant of slack, then just as quickly take up the slack and the proper attitude or angle in the rod after the fish reenters the water.

Some species, notably salmon, larger brown trout, and the like, will try to conserve their energy not by running and jumping but by either headshaking, side to side, grinding the hook into the gravel or by simply "grabbing the bottom" and sulking. *Keep that fish moving.* Wear it down quickly. If it won't move, try hitting the base of your reel seat with the palm of your hand. The shock waves traveling up the rod and down the line will usually get him moving, fast.

Above all, enjoy it! The reading, the gear, the preparation, the trip, the casting and strike *all lead up to this moment!* Play the fish, long enough to tire it and land it but not so long as to lose it, exhausted, downstream, past the point of sport or survival.

Landing

As the fish starts to tire and become played out, take up line and ease him into a quieter stretch of water. Expect at least one more jolt of energy as it gets close to you. Keep your hand on the rod's grip as you guide it toward the net. Resist the temptation to slide your hand up the rod as this negates the cushioning effect of the rod's arc and can strain both tippet and rod tip. Don't "scoop up" your fish, instead *ease* the fish into a half submerged net *headfirst* or gently grab it around the middle. I always instinctively wet my hand first if I'm not using a net. A dry hand can remove the protective slime from a fish's body, subjecting it to disease and unnecessarily stress a fish that you plan to release. A fish usually doesn't have to be lifted from the water, particularly with a barbless hook. A quick twist and shake of the hook will usually free it. If not, a pair of forceps or small needlenose pliers can be used to grab the hook's shank and twist it loose.

Fly-fishing usually hooks the fish in the lip or jaw, but occasionally, particularly when using nymphs, a fish may be hooked in the tongue, or the hook may penetrate through its mouth and into the eye area. Use your judgment. If a *legal* fish is bleeding freely or mortally injured, then keep it, for it'll only turn up downstream, dead, later on. I've also found that if it is necessary to lift a fish from the water to remove a badly embedded hook, it can be done much more easily by turning the fish upside down.

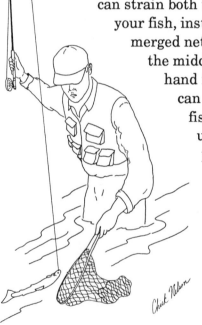

▲ *Ease the fish into the submerged net, head first.*

This tends to subdue, calm or disorient it for the few seconds necessary to extricate the hook.

If you're planning to release your fish, *don't throw it back* in the literal sense, but *place* it back. Put the fish in the water, cradling it until it remains upright. An overly tired fish needs to regain its strength *and* equilibrium. Hold it in a gentle current or slowly move it back and forth for as long as it takes to get the gill plates moving again. It will quickly dart from your hands when ready.

I was up on Hat Creek one year and was impressed to see a fellow take a break from his fishing to tie and match the hatch that was coming off that morning. A quick passing look at the size #18 or #20 fly he had tied showed that he not only matched the size, color and form of the emerging duns but was an accomplished fly-tier. I was even more impressed when a few minutes later I noticed

A brown trout takes a few seconds for a photo opportunity. ▼

▲ *Fish On!*

him fast to a nice fish, that I estimated to be in the 15–16" range. Then my impression changed. He proceeded to play that fish for well over 15 minutes, taking up line and *letting it out again as the fish tired,* just to prolong the fight. He then simply unhooked the exhausted rainbow making no attempt to revive it and let it drift out in the current. I doubt that it survived. A fish *successfully* released today is around to strike and fight another day!

Is It Wild?

If, however, you intend to keep a few fish for lunch or dinner, then plan it. It's no secret that many lakes and streams are managed on what is called a "put and take" system. This means that planted fish, reared at a hatchery, are put in with the full expectation that they'll be caught. Statistics also show that many, if not most, of these planted fish are neither wily enough nor genetically suited for survival, beyond the season that they're planted. Sure, some do make it through the winter season and these "holdover" fish eventually become almost as good fighters as the natives. There is even a concern about mixing these genetically watered-down fish in the same waters with wild fish as they may dilute the strain. Arguments on that score aside, if you've decided to keep a few fish, keep a planted one and release the wild ones. Most states' fishing regulations include drawings that illustrate the key features to distinguish the differences between the two.

The rays in the dorsal fin of a wild fish are usually straight and not bent or distorted. The adipose fin is usually clipped for identification or snubbed off, from the close proximity of being raised in a hatchery pen. Coloration is not nearly as vivid on hatchery fish nor are the *plant*s as lively fighters as the wild fish. Prepared correctly, however, these plants make fine eating and will be far fresher than any store or restaurant fish you've ever eaten, many of which were farm raised anyhow.

To maximize the taste of your fish, do a couple of things. First, if the fishing is good, and you're regularly catching

Rays on Dorsal Fin of a hatchery fish may be bent, crooked or completely rubbed off (top), while a wild fish's is straight.

Adipose Fin of a hatchery fish may be clipped or snubbed off (top), while a wild fish's is intact.

A fall-run steelhead ready to be released back into a coastal stream.

fish throughout the day, try to plan your "keeper" close to mealtime. Land your fish quickly so that excessive enzymes do not invade the flesh. Also, gut, clean and remove the fish's gills as soon as practical after the catch. A small, sharp pocketknife comes in handy for this chore. Put your catch in either a wicker creel or in a wet, canvas type creel that cools by evaporation. Some wet grass set between the fish helps the cooling process. Going back to the timing of catch versus cooking, don't leave the fish in the creel or in the hot sun so long as to ruin the catch past the point of usability and waste the fish.

Grilled, poached or fried trout or panfish, cooked over an open fire, in a remote setting, tastes better than any fancy uptown restaurant. Remember though, *catch your limit but limit your kill!*

THE REST OF THE STORY...

Knots
— A Dozen⁺ Favorites

6

*T*he first simple knots have been with us since early
man tried to join together two pieces of vine. Through the
centuries, stories from Alexander the Great's cutting of the
Gordian knot, to become master of Asia, to the artful
drawing of ancient mariners' knots have shown us the
ingenuity and variety of knots tied for specific purposes.

First, as a fisherman and now fly fisher, knowing how
to tie a selection of good, strong, workable knots is a must.
Knots connect backing to reel, backing to line, line to
leader, leader to tippet to fly. Tie the wrong knot, tie it
poorly or hastily, and you're going to lose fish. (Uninten-
tionally putting a "wind knot" in your leader will have the
same effect.) And when you do, Murphy's Law will make
sure that it will be *a good one*, for the small ones rarely
tax your connections.

There are three elements in the knots we're about to
learn. First, the *right knot* for the right application;
second, *tying the knot properly t*o maximize its strength-
maintaining qualities; and last, *not negating numbers one
and two by tying it dry* and allowing excessive heat or
friction to weaken the monofilament.

Let's start with a basic premise. A piece of braided line
or monofilament is strongest before a knot is put into it
(unless doubled or reinforced in some way). Therefore, we
need to avoid putting any additional knots where they
don't belong; i.e., wind knots in your leader. Such a knot
can reduce the strength, at that juncture, by 50%, sometimes more. Therefore, you may think that you're fighting

a large fish with a 3 lb. test tippet when, given a wind knot in the 3 lb. section, you have reduced its strength by half—this is assuming that the tippet is fresh and it has not been damaged in any other way (frays, nicks, etc.). To prove this to yourself, try a simple test: pull a knotted tippet and watch *where* and *how easily* it will break.

Also, we should not tie anymore knots than needed into the line and should choose those that retain the best strength, say 85–90%.

What follows is a series of illustrations, applications and instructions for tying a baker's dozen of those knots that you'll need to know to assemble your tackle and those that you'll use most often when fishing.

∎ *Backing line to fly reel* —

Run the end of the backing line through the front of the fly reel, around the spool's arbor, and out again. Tie a simple overhand knot to its end, draw it tight, and trim it closely. Using this "tag" end of the line, tie another overhand knot around the main line. Pull it tight, drawing and working it close to the first knot (which will act as a stopper). Now, lubricate the mainline with a little saliva and pull it so the noose is snug against the arbor.

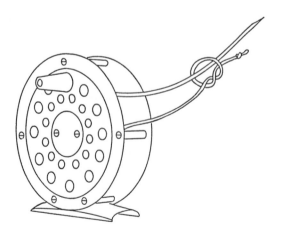

█ *Clinch Knots:* *quick, neat connectors for flies.*

Single Clinch — Pass the end of the leader or tippet
material through the eye of the hook and wrap the end
over the standing part of the line several times. Slide the
tag end back through the opening formed between the first
wrap and the eye. Lubricate it with a little saliva and
slowly pull tight.

Improved Clinch — Proceed as above, but after the tag
end is inserted through the first opening, pass it back
through the loop just formed. Moisten and tighten with
steady pressure.

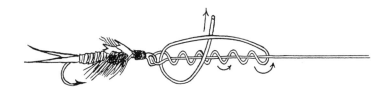

Double Clinch — Pass the end of the leader/tippet
material through the eye of the *hook twice* and wrap the
tag end over the standing line several times. Slide the
tag end back *through both loops* at the opening formed

between the first wrap and the eye of the hook. Moisten and slowly pull tight.

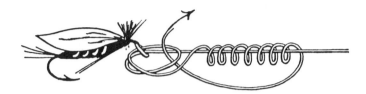

■ *Double Turle knot — for a straight-line pull from leader to fly and for use on either upturned or downturned eyed hooks.*

Pass the tag end of the leader/tippet through the eye of the fly. Slide the fly several inches down the line. Assuming you're right-handed (reverse if left-handed), hold the tag end with fingers of the right hand and wrap the leader material around your index and middle fingers twice to form two loops. The tag end is then passed under and around both loops and a double, overhand knot is formed. Holding the double loop at the overhand knot, slide the fly down the line and through the double loop. The moistened loop is then slowly drawn tight at the head of the fly, the knot seating itself *neatly behind the hook's eye.*

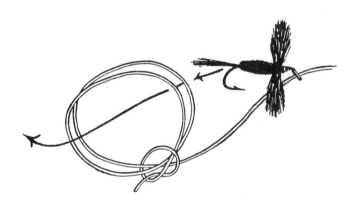

■ *Albright knot* — *the preferred knot for connecting light monofilament too heavy, and connecting backing to line.*

Form a double loop in the line. Place the tag end of the backing or leader material (depending on the application) through the loop as shown in the illustration and make six to eight turns over the standing loop. Insert and trap the tag end of the backing/leader through the end of the loop. Slowly pull the moistened turns tight, working the coils down *neatly and evenly* to the end of the line loop, and trim.

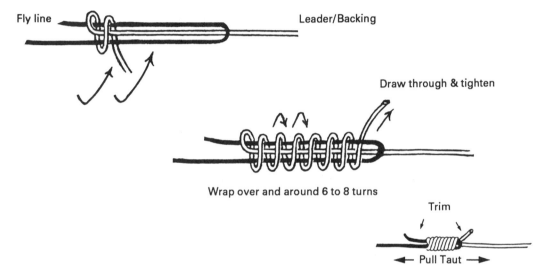

Fly line   Leader/Backing

Draw through & tighten

Wrap over and around 6 to 8 turns

Trim

← Pull Taut →

■ *Nail/Tube knot* — *a connector knot for joining back to fly line, fly line to leader, etc.*

Lay six to seven inches of line and leader parallel to each other. Place a small diameter nail, plastic tube, or similar object between the line and leader. While holding the line, leader, and nail together with the thumb and forefinger of one hand, wrap the tag end of the leader over and around the line, nail (tube), and the leader itself six to eight times. The tag end is then inserted back through the opening that is formed by the nail (or pass the leader through the tube). Withdraw the nail/tube and slowly draw the coils tight. Pull on all four strands at first; then, when the slack has been taken out of the coils and the coils are neatly parallel to each other (avoid overlaps), pull tight and trim.

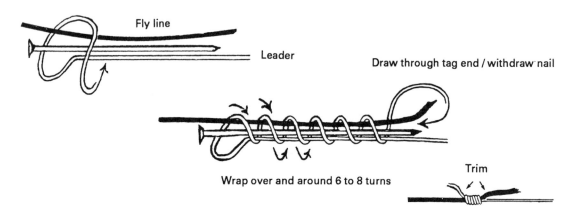

Fly line

Leader

Draw through tag end / withdraw nail

Wrap over and around 6 to 8 turns

Trim

▌ *Blood/Barrel knot* — *an essential knot in building tapered leaders, mending leaders / lines, leader to tippet connections, etc.*

Wind one leader strand three or four times around the standing part of the second line. Insert the tag end back behind the first turn. Do the same with the other leader end, inserting its tag end through in the opposite direction, lubricate and slowly pull tight.

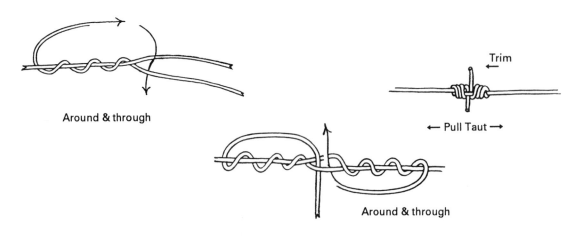

Around & through

Trim

← Pull Taut →

Around & through

■ *Dropper Extension* — If an extension dropper is to be formed, allow yourself six to seven inches of extra leader material from the *heavier* of the two materials (to minimize tangles). This longer end becomes the "dropper" line for attaching the second fly. Trim the other tag end.

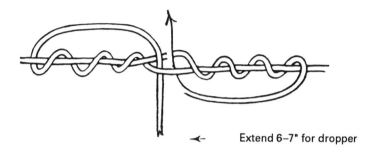

Extend 6–7" for dropper

■ *Dropper Loop* — *a connector loop for attaching an additional fly or lure.*

Form a two to three inch loop in the line. Wrap this section of the line overhand through the loop three or four times. Now, bring the mid-section of the remaining loop up and through the twisted strands and draw the two ends tight.

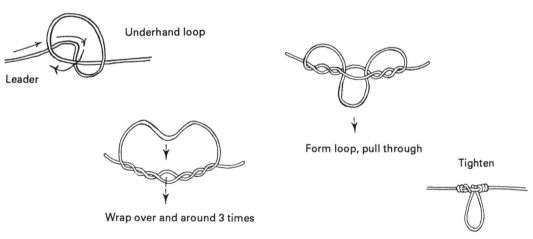

Underhand loop

Leader

Form loop, pull through

Tighten

Wrap over and around 3 times

■ *Figure-Eight knot* — *This is a fast and easy knot to tie but is best used with braided wire, necessary for some saltwater situations.*

Pass the wire through the hook's eye and around the standing part of the wire. Insert the tag end through the loop formed in front of the hook-eye. Tighten and trim with cutting pliers.

Draw through & tighten

 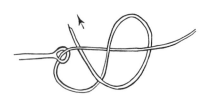

■ Surgeon's knot — *best for lines of unequal diameter: line to leader, leader to tippet, line to line connections, etc.*

Overlap the ends of the line to be joined and tie a simple overhand knot, tied through the same loop twice, or three times for greater strength. Moisten, slowly tighten, and trim.

Trim

←— Pull Taut —→

Fly line and leader

Leader

Fly line

Form overhand loop, pull through 2 to 3 times

■ Duncan Loop — *The loop or uni-knot enhances the action of the wet-fly or nymph and thereby lets it act more natural.*

Begin by passing the tippet end of the leader through the hook's eye. Take 6 to 8 inches of the tag end and form a loop parallel to the standing line. Next, take the tag end and pass it around the standing end of the line four of five times. Moisten the line and draw the coils tight, leaving an open "loop" at the hook's eye for the fly to freely move.

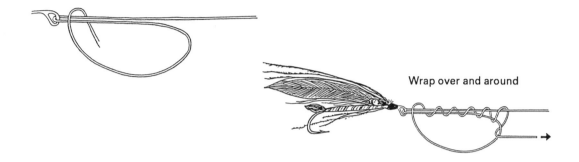

Wrap over and around

▌*Perfection Loop* — *for use either at the butt end of a leader to be joined to a fly line with a spliced loop or at the terminal end of a leader for quick changing of pre-tied saltwater fly rigs.*

Take four or five inches of the tag end of the leader and form the first loop by passing the tag end behind the standing part, or stem of the leader. Pass the tag end around the stem a second time and back behind the loop thus formed. As shown in the illustration, the second, middle loop, is drawn up and through the first loop and tightened.

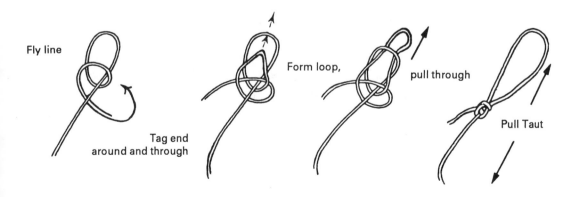

Fly line

Tag end around and through

Form loop,

pull through

Pull Taut

Once your reels are set up, with backing, fly line and leader, the most frequently used knots will be those used to attach leader to fly line and to tie on your fly. *Thoroughly commit these to memory.*

Practice some of these knots at home, using a couple of pieces of light rope or heavy cord to get the feeling for what is going on. Once you have it down pat, try it with some monofilament fishing line or leader material *at home* rather than under the pressure of being at the water's edge—where you'll surely rather be fishing than trying to hastily tie a reliable knot with trembling fingers!

Remember, when tying each knot, to lubricate it as you snug it tight. A little saliva, water, or floatant paste prevents excessive heat and friction and helps it slide together more uniformly and more easily. Also, *guiding the wraps on each knot while smoothly pulling it taut* assures that turns, that can weaken it, are not laid over one another, other than those for which it was designed. Carefully trim the tag end to avoid the line from getting hung up on the loose stub, but leave a slight margin for assurance against slippage. There is one application in which I never feel comfortable using silicone line dressing as a lubricant, and that is at the connection of tippet to the fly. In fact, I'm very careful to avoid dressing the fly, and then, with some silicone still remaining on my fingertips, tie on a fly. I have had more than one incident of losing a good fish to a bad knot — and I suspect that the slick silicone was probably a contributing factor. Some can argue against this, but frankly I'd rather be sure and use a little saliva instead.

Check your leader periodically for knots, "wind" or otherwise, and cut it back or replace it as frequently as needed. Periodically run your leader through your fingers to feel for any nicks or abrasions. Also, check your other connections for wear or fraying. *You'll remember a lost fish longer than a landed one* and no one will see or believe you hooked it but you. *A minute checking your knots is time well spent!*

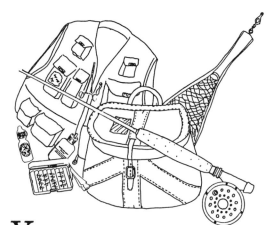

Y**ou may have seen** the cartoon that's circulated about the fly angler outfitted from head to toe with every conceivable gadget on the marketplace and an enumeration by item of its pricing. The cartoon character was better armed than a modern combat soldier and cost as much to outfit. The point being that you can overdo it, equipment-wise, in fly-fishing as much or maybe more so than in other sports. An old adage is that certain lures and "equipment" are sold to catch fisherman not the fish! Our cartoon character's buying spree is also detrimental to his health for he'll sink like a rock if he ever gets near the water.

Let's put together a list of the basics, the bare minimum needed to take a fish, and add on from there as needed. Let's also try do keep in mind what we need versus what we want. Let's face it, it's fun to buy. There is definitely something to be said about the anticipation and vicarious pleasure of picking up "stuff" off-season as it adds to the involvement in the sport. Also, many of the available accessories do serve a useful purpose, perhaps not essential, but to facilitate the performance of a specific task... *Now, there's just the rationale we needed to justify our next purchase!*

Bare Bones

You can get away with as little as a fly rod, a reel filled with the correct line, some leader material and a handful of flies. This will raise some fish, however it is a little too basic for most people. So let's see what else there is...

Accessories

The "vest" is to the fly-fisher what the glove is to the baseball player...you can play the game without it, but it sure won't be much fun!

A decent *fly-fishing vest* is a traveling, wearable file "system" that not only holds just about everything you'll need for a day's outing (and often too much more) but if filled with some forethought, organizes each item and tool where it is easily and readily available. I find that a fly vest is invaluable in holding and organizing my equipment for a day's outing, even if I'm fishing from a canoe or raft. Within its numerous pockets I can store a wide assortment of goodies that I'll use during the course of the day.

For years vests were of a standard cotton poplin design with a multitude of pockets. However, in the last few years new fabrications, closure materials, assorted lengths for specialized fishing techniques, component vest "systems" and the like have entered the marketplace. A quality vest is a worthwhile investment as it's comfortable to wear all day even when fully "loaded." It's number, size and arrangement of pockets, D-Rings and pouches will be thoughtfully laid out, constructed of and sewn with high quality materials that will provide years of life.

In shopping for a vest look for features like self-healing nylon zippers, preferably with large tabs that are easy to find and grasp, pockets that have flaps secured by Velcro® or similar hook and loop tape to prevent loss of equipment, and a design that distributes the weight of the vest evenly across the shoulders, not on the back of the neck. Avoid vests that have buttons or snaps as pocket closures, as these are unreliable and difficult to close when using one hand.

The better manufacturers incorporate all these features whereas the cheaper, low-end imports do not. Try the vest on, considering its fit, as it may be worn over a heavy shirt or sweater. Make sure that it doesn't bind as you move and mimic the movements of a cast. Look at the different models to determine which has the number and layout of pockets best suited to your intended fishing needs. Color? A personal choice, but you'll want something that allows you to blend in with the environment yet is comfortable. Greens work well in this regard, but subdued greys and tans can be a lot cooler in hot, sunny climates. This is your judgement call.

There are a number of alternatives to the fly vest, from multi-flap-pocketed shirts to a variety of chest packs that are specifically designed for this purpose. Among the best designs is the WoodRiver® bag. You may feel "out of uniform" at first when employing a bag, but "bags" are actually more traditional tackle carriers of fly-fishing gear, vests being introduced only in the last 30–40 years.

The WoodRiver® bag is built of heavy duty nylon pack-cloth, supported by rigid inserts, that can be removed to fold the bag flat. The interior of the bag (depending on model) has an assortment of pouches and dividers to hold everything from fly boxes, floatant, spare reels to a small camera. The exterior needlework lays out pockets and pouches that will hold everything from your fly-vise to a rain jacket and anything in between. There are also a number of D-rings for attaching a landing net and the like, as well as a four-strap system that really sets this bag apart from the singular, old-world, over the shoulder variety. Depending on water depth and personal prefer-ence, you can wear the bag comfortably hung around your waist, either behind or to the side, where it can be swung around to the front to reveal its contents, or it can be worn chest-high in front for deep wading. All and all a viable option to the vest.

While we're on the subject of vests and alternate tackle carriers, it might be fun to assess what we'll want to put in them, before we tackle the subject of waders.

Fly boxes are one of the first accessory items that you'll buy. There are dozens of different types on the market, the majority being made of plastic or aluminum, in a range of sizes. You'll develop your own preferences soon

enough. Be aware, however, that your dry-flies need to have their hackle protected from being crushed. To this end, boxes with individual compartments, as well as those types with clips and/or foam, to hold your flies upright, are necessary. You can get away with one such box, at first, that will hold your dry-flies, as well as some nymphs and wets, or you could pick up a combination box that has compartments for your dry-flies on one side and clips/foam on the other. You should remember to dry out your flies before putting them back in the box or rust can develop on the lot. I usually take all the fly boxes out of my vest at the end of the day, open their lids and lay them out in the sun on my truck's dashboard to thoroughly dry them out. This may seem like I'm being overly cautious, but when you have forty or fifty flies in one box, you'll want to take a few minutes to protect your investment.

Fly floatant comes in a couple of forms, either the spray-on variety or in a silicone paste. Either is invaluable in redressing a poorly floating fly, the latter serving double duty to dress your floating fly line. I'll carry both, generally using the spray to either "touch-up" a fly or for use on my smallest flies that don't require heavy dressing. There are solutions available that require the fly to be thoroughly soaked for a few minutes and then allowed to dry. These I consider "pre-trip" preparations.

There are also compounds available that, when applied to a wet-fly or nymph, will expedite it sinking, although a little mud smeared on a fly will usually work nicely.

Desiccant "crystals" such as Super Dry Fly™ and the like are useful in cleaning and drawing all the moisture out of a saturated dry-fly prior to redressing it with floatant. This can be very useful when a dry-fly is floating poorly, a fly change is impractical because of low light conditions or if it's the only fly you have left the fish are hitting!

A small *nail-clipper* or line clipper specifically designed for the fisherman aids greatly in clipping a new knot or in trimming a fly. The nippers designed specifically for the fly-fisher usually incorporate a needle for cleaning out the hook's eye and any other number of features from a small whetstone to a nail-knot tying tool.

Mini-retractors. These are enclosed reels about the size of a quarter that contain about a foot of braided line, attached to a spring mechanism. They fasten to your vest by means of a pin-clip. A couple of these strategically placed on your vest, will hold either your clippers, stream thermometer, or paste floatant allowing easy access to them without digging through your pockets and preventing their loss.

A safety pin. I had one pinned to a flap on my vest for years and found it invaluable for cleaning glue from the eye of a fly or in opening up a (occasional) wind-knot. As mentioned, there are clippers available now that incorporate a needle in their design for just such a purpose.

A hemostat or forceps can be very helpful in extricating a small or deeply embedded hook from a fish's mouth quickly and safely. I usually just clip the end to my shirt or pocket flap of my vest where it's handiest.

A small whetstone or file will put a sharp point on a new hook or recondition a hook dulled by bumping along the river's bottom.

A few spools of *tippet material* in assorted sizes/ breaking test strength are very useful to maximize the range of delicacy of your presentation as well as extend the life of a leader tip that has been cut back.

Lead is useful in getting your fly down to the fish's level. Twist-on, split-spot, fuse lead all work and you'll soon develop your own preferences. Moldable soft lead is also available but my experience is that it is not dense enough for its size and tends to work its way off my leader rather quickly.

A small stainless steel *needlenose pliers*, is a great aid in pressing down the hook's barb and for squeezing on split shot as well as straightening out or off-setting a hook's point.

Small scissors or a small Swiss army knife with its assortment of tools is also handy for trimming flies or yarn. A small folding knife is useful for a multitude of uses right down to cleaning an occasional fish for a meal.

Strike-indicator yarn is very helpful when fishing nymphs in moving water. A bright-colored tuft of yarn or other indicator can signal a subtle strike and is especially useful when learning to nymph fish, or when glare or rough water makes it difficult to follow your line's drift.

A **wading staff** should be considered for all stream conditions that involve swift and/or deep water. A fixed wood staff or ski pole will do, but one of the collapsible folding types is much more convenient. Somewhat cumbersome to carry, a good wading staff is insurance against getting stuck or unstuck from a bad situation while crossing or negotiating fast water or slippery bottoms. A wading staff is also helpful in probing your next footing and, acting as a third leg, can stabilize and support you while setting yourself up into a casting position to a prime lie that you might otherwise have to pass up. Like all insurance, you'll question why you're carrying it when you don't need it, but you don't need it 'till you need it, as they say.

Leader/Tippet dispensers are very useful in keeping your tippet material neatly organized in one convenient location. They are light, compact, eliminate tangles and the bulk of carrying several individual spools.

Leader maker tools are handy for quickly and easily tying perfect blood knots and custom designing your own tapers to assure optimum fly turn-over.

Vest-pocket lights of the gooseneck or "bite-light" variety are also popular and I carried one for a few years for those occasions when a hatch at dusk could mean changing flies in poor light. I eventually found myself not using the light that I carried since it didn't offer enough light to be of any real help. Now, if the fishing is that good at dusk, I either clean and ready a fly taken by a fish via some Super Dry Fly™ crystals or hold a new fly up to the

sky's fading light and tie on a new one. Once it's too dark to do that (and I've done it against some quickly dimming backgrounds) I'll call it quits, for the night. You may find that a small flashlight, tucked in a pocket, for finding your way back to your car or camp, is more useful. Light or not it's a personal choice.

Landing net. To use one or not, that is the question. Some catch and release proponents don't carry one as a sign of their statement not to keep or kill fish. Personally I think you can more easily land and control a fish, without doing it harm by either ill-handling or excessively tiring the fish out, while bringing it to submission by using a net. If you do use one I suggest buying one with a shallow cotton (not nylon) net as it will less likely abrade the fish or get hung up in its gills. A key-chain type retractor, fastened between the vest and the net's clip, will be a great aid in drawing the net under the fish without completely detaching it from the vest. Also, I've found that if you carry your net, out of the way on the back of the vest, tuck the net portion into the waistband of your safety belt to secure it. This will keep it from getting hung up on the bushes. If you choose not to use a net and plan to release your fish, then barbless hooks will greatly aid you in expeditiously releasing a fish by a quick turn of the hook without lifting the fish from its watery home.

Net retractor. As noted above, attached between your net's handle and one of the rings on your vest (usually in back), it simplifies holding and handling your net without having to completely unhook it when landing a fish.

Scale vs. tape measure. Again, if you plan to release a fish, a scale will be detrimental to its health, as taking the fish out of the water and hanging it from its gill cover will likely cause it permanent injury. A tape measure or *tape mark on your rod* is the quickest and easiest way to measure a fish before letting it go. But…be advised, if it looks like 18" or 2 pounds, then it is. If on the other hand you measure or weigh it and it "shrinks," then you can't call it

what you now know it's not. And fish do tend to "shrink" when put to the test!

Next, we'll assume that beyond fishing from shore or from a water craft, wading bare, that is, in shorts or jeans, generally can only be done comfortably for short periods or in warm water conditions. The latter is not too often encountered in the cold water environment necessary for most trout. Therefore, **waders** or **hip boots** border on being a necessity. These can be of either the bootfoot variety, that is with boots attached, or the more versatile stocking-foot variety. The latter are composed of latex, closed-cell neoprene, coated nylon or the like, adult versions of "Doctor Denton's" (without the trap door!). Completely waterproof (when new) the stocking-foot hippers or waders require the addition of wading shoes or the equivalent. Given the laced/Velcro® closure of the separate shoe, stocking-foot waders offer more ankle support, better fit, and consequently, better stability in and around the water. Also, wading shoes, specifically designed for stocking-foot waders, almost always come from the manufacturer with either a **felt sole** and/or **cleats** which greatly enhance their rock holding ability or they can be retrofitted with same.

Personally, although I like the few places I can wear hip boots and love how cool they feel on a hot day, I always find myself tettering on my toes because I'm about to flood their tops. Also in the event of a downpour, a rain jacket will run the water right into the tops of hip boots.

Another pointer, for what it's worth. A while back, I started wearing sweat pants under my waders. I find these give me better insulation against the cold water, and a greater range of movement than with stiff jeans that bind and negate the advantage of stretchy, latex waders. Conversely, under my neoprene waders I'll wear either polypropylene long-johns or stretch, work-out-type tights. This is because the neoprenes are so form-fitting that pants don't fit well under them and shorts feel too clammy.

In the same breath with waders, I'll also include a wader *safety belt* with a *quick-release* buckle. Secured snugly around your waist, the safety belt prevents the rapid filling of the waders in the inevitable event of a dunking. *This is a necessity!* You definitely don't want to be stuck in your waders, anchored by a dozen gallons of water, heading downstream. This is a cold and potentially life-threatening situation.

There is also a new item that's entered the market in the last few years, that is a quick-inflating set of *safety suspenders*. In the event of a sudden dunking, this flotation collar is activated by a quick pull on the CO_2 cartridge handle. The manufacturer claims to have designed these after helplessly losing a friend to drowning. It has been reported to have saved several lives already in its brief entrance into the market, and it is worth checking into.

Sunglasses. There are two primary reasons for a flyfisher to wear sunglasses: *safety* and for *seeing fish* and their lies more clearly.

The safety factor falls into two broad categories. The first is that the glass acts as a barrier to protect your eyes from an errant fly, your's or someone else's. The  implications of a sharp hook flying through the air are obvious and although not a fool-proof defense, sunglasses or regular glasses for that matter, go a long way in protecting the eyes from a frontal assault. Sunglasses can be further broken down into *prescription* and "regular" or "polarized." The latter lenses will sort out and selectively reduce light density by filtering and admitting only parallel light rays to pass at a given angle, something like looking through a set of venetian blinds, thereby reducing "glare." Conventional lenses, however, simply reduce light *intensity* as it passes through the lenses. There's even agreement that darker, nonpolarized lenses, allow the eye's pupil to dilate in order to "see," thus making the eye vulnerable to damage by ambient ultraviolet rays. Eye strain and fatigue are lessened considerably by the use of polarized lenses.

In the second regard, you cannot locate, nor fish to, what you can't see. Sunglasses and polarized lenses, in particular, cut the brightness from the water and enable you to more easily and comfortably search for holding and feeding lies. Polarized lenses will allow you to almost see *into* the water by dramatically reducing the glare. This allows you to follow the drift of your fly and/or leader as it approaches a fish that you can then see rise to your fly! Additionally, your enhanced ability to see will help you safely wade from one sure-footed casting position to the next.

The selection of sunglasses will be an individual choice as to fit, style, and budget but shop the market thoroughly before you buy. There are lightweight plastic lenses and slightly heavier but more durable scratch-resistant glass lenses, clip-on's, models with snap-on side shields to ward off stray light, flip-ups, and designs with clear lenses or magnifying lenses at the bottom half of the frame. I'm sure bifocals also can be ground by your local optician.

Choose your sunglasses well as they are a valuable part of your equipment and protect your investment by wearing one of the many **safety cords** that secure them around your neck.

There is something else that I find very helpful: a check list. Before I take off for a weekend fishing trip, rather than try and remember if I have everything I need, I refer to *"the list."* This not only saves time and energy but has the obvious, proven advantage of assuring me that I don't leave behind something that I'll need.

I keep my wife's and my own wading gear in one medium size canvas bag. Waders, hippers, safety belt, wading staff, shoes and the like all go into this "wet" bag. The equipment is then dried out after each trip, the latex waders turned inside out and powdered, repairs made, as needed, and put away ready for the next trip.

The reels, leaders, spare fly boxes and other sundry

stuff, that is not kept in our vests is stored in a second, compartmentalized, carry-on type bag. Basically all we have to do is grab the "wet bag," vests, rod cases and equipment bag and we know it's all there. (Although I always go through my "checklist" to be sure!)

Rain Jacket. Sooner or later you're going to need one. If you confine your fishing to warm, sunny, summer days, an occasional shower may not bother you. If you pursue the sport further, you'll undoubtedly be fishing virtually year-round in all kinds of weather. That being the case, getting caught without any protection could potentially subject you to hypothermia. A rain jacket, tucked away in the rear pocket of your fly vest when the weather looks threatening, is worth having along. An attached hood with a visor will keep the rain off your head and your face or glasses. Some of the better models were specially designed with pockets and closures for the fly-fisher. Combine these features with a waterproof, breathable fabric, such as Ultrex®, and you'll have a piece of equipment you can take from Alaska to the tropics. Be aware also that in a thunderstorm a fly rod, particularly a

With the protection of the proper rain gear, you'll hardly notice the weather. ▼

graphite one, is a potential lightening rod, so head for appropriate shelter until it passes.

A couple of years back I was fishing a section of the McCloud River when the weather turned ugly. Either the change in the barometric pressure and/or the rain knocking insects into the water really turned the fish on. There were rises everywhere and I had a hook-up every third or fourth cast. As the lightening storm worsened, I found myself side-casting to keep my rod tip low, timing each cast between the lightening strikes. I did this for about fifteen minutes until I couldn't stand the tension any longer and snapped to my senses. The fabulous fishing just wasn't worth my life. *(Although I'm sure that there could be worse ways to go!)*

Plan ahead—

Just as a checklist is an invaluable aid as a pre-trip guide, so are a few elementary phone calls before you leave. Check with local fly and tackle shops in the area you plan to fish about water conditions, any hatches or other activity that may be occurring and perhaps local weather conditions. These people are generally very willing and able to supply you with useful, up-to-the-minute information and suggestions on fly patterns that are working best. If it's a holiday weekend, think about reserving a motel room or campsite to avoid a last minute hassle when you arrive. If it's an unfamiliar area, get the proper maps and/or directions to where you want to go. Check with the district Fish and Game Department and the Forest Service and Bureau of Land Management Offices for copies of their maps which are available at a nominal charge, either in person or by mail. If you're planning to take a boat, canoe, pram or float tube, check on local regulations as to whether motorized craft are allowed, if you can fish from such a floating device (in some states it's not permitted) and where the best access points are in and *out* of the water.

In short, leave as little to chance in the planning as

CHECKLIST

The items listed below are personal choices, offered as a guide, but you might consider these in your own experimentation with equipment.

Bare Bones Basics

- [ ] rod
- [ ] reel/fly line/backing
- [ ] leaders
- [ ] fly boxes/flies
- [ ] line clipper/nippers
- [ ] license
- [ ] safety pin
- [ ] _____

Helpful Additions

- [ ] fly vest
- [ ] fly floatant (spray or paste)
- [ ] retrievers to hold clippers, etc.
- [ ] wading staff
- [ ] Swiss army knife
- [ ] file or hook sharpening stone
- [ ] spare leaders/tippet material
- [ ] twist-on or splitshot lead
- [ ] forceps/hemostat
- [ ] waders/boots/safety belt or hip boots
- [ ] landing net
- [ ] strike-indicators
- [ ] sunglasses/hat

- [ ] creel
- [ ] rain jacket
- [ ] spare reel/spool
- [ ] small water-resistant camera
- [ ] stream thermometer
- [ ] desiccant drying crystals
- [ ] small needlenose pliers
- [ ] additional fly boxes
- [ ] tippet dispenser
- [ ] spare reel or spool with different line
- [ ] leader-tying tool
- [ ] insect repellent
- [ ] small flashlight

Specialty

- [ ] float tube/pram
- [ ] fly-tying kit

- [ ] shooting taper line
- [ ] _____

possible for you'll find that in the infinite pleasure of fly-fishing the time goes by all too quickly and you don't want to minimize that precious time further by running around looking for a place to stay or gain access to the water.

Keep a Log

After everything that we've talked about, it sounds like the last thing you need to do is to carry a notebook—and you don't, at least not on your person (although some people do). At the day's end, however, while your thoughts are still fresh, review what happened, what worked and what didn't work. Commercial fly-fishing logs are available through mail order or retail, but any small notebook will work. A diary can be invaluable as a reference for future trips. It can outline what conditions were present on a certain piece of water in any given year and enable you to duplicate your success and take a shortcut past those things that were a waste of time.

▼ *First entry for the fishing log...*

A diary should have several major and minor categories as outlined. These help pinpoint either location, weather/water conditions, technique, flies and a record of your catch. It serves not only as a graphic reminder of your trip but also any extraneous issues as to ideal time, hatches, types of fish present, etc., will help you fine tune your ability for repeated success.

FISHING LOG

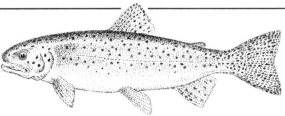

Date _____

Location _____ Specific Section _____

Type of water fished:
☐ Riffle ☐ Pocket ☐ Runs ☐ Rock gardens
☐ Pools ☐ Headwaters ☐ _____

Water level: ☐ High ☐ Low ☐ Normal
☐ Clear ☐ Off Color

Weather: ☐ ☐ ☐

☐ ☐ ☐ _____ Air° _____ Water° _____

Observations:
Insect activity/hatches _____ Time _____ Type _____ Duration _____

Feeding activity/Rise forms: _____

Fly line used: ☐ Floating ☐ Sink-tip ☐ Sinking ☐

Method fished: ☐ Wets ☐ Drys ☐ Nymphs ☐ Streamers ☐ Terrestrials ☐ Popping bugs ☐ _____

Fishing activity: No. of strikes _____ No. landed _____ Best Pattern(s) _____ Size _____

   Trout: ☐ Rainbow ☐ Brown ☐ Brook ☐ Cutthroat ☐ _____ ☐ _____

   Other: ☐ Smallmouth Bass ☐ Largemouth Bass ☐ Panfish ☐ _____ ☐ _____

Best fish: _____"/lbs _____ **Average fish:** _____"/lbs _____ **Type** _____

Best times: _____ **Slowest times:** _____

Things to remember to do and to bring for the next time:
_____
_____

Excess items to leave behind:
_____

Comments:
_____
_____

NOTES

Map Drawings, Reference Points, etc.

Nickle **8**
Knowledge

*I*f you're resolute in improving your skills as a fly-fisher, then you are inevitably going to catch fish on a regular basis. Often times, except for certain limited conditions, you'll be able to *outsmart* the fish and *outfish* the other folks that are using lures and bait. Therefore, given the obvious in terms of local and state regulations, you'll have to limit your catch, be it in size or in number.

In many streams today, "catch and release" *is* the law, because of the depletion of the environment necessary to support a sustaining population of fish or due to the accessibility and related pressure on a given area. Couple this with a world-wide demand on fish stocks and the almost hard to believe, virtually unregulated gill-net and drift-net ocean practices that are plundering our oceans resources, in general and anadromous species in particular, an awareness and consciousness to the need for catch and release fishing is gaining in popularity.

All your acquired skills will be used to hook and land a fish. The fish's release, *unharmed,* will educate the fish to some degree and make it wiser for the next angler...and the *next angler could well be you!* By releasing all or most of your day's catch, you will help to perpetuate the resource *and* the sport for all that follow, thereby increasing the enjoyment of all and, in the greater scope, forming a larger base from which to voice our concern for ill-planned wildlife management practices.

For a fish to expect to eat an insect, or other foodstuff, but instead finds itself fast to an artificial fly and line, is cause for both surprise and trauma. The inherent struggle and effort to fight both line and current can quickly tire most fish. (The inherent struggle and excitement of a large fish can also quickly tire a fisherman, but that's another story!) An exhausted fish must be expeditiously unhooked, revived and quickly returned to the water, if it is to survive. To that end there are a number of things that you can do to assure its chance of survival.

Catch & Release

Fly-fishing, as opposed to bait or lure fishing, serves "catch and release" fishing best simply because, in most instances, the fish is hooked either in the mouth, lip or jaw. Rarely is the hook swallowed or deeply embedded in the throat or other vital area. Barbless hooks, available commercially or "de-barbed" by simply pressing down the barb with a small needlenose pliers, make hook removal fast and easy and offer a quicker release than the barbed version.

Barbed   **De-barbed**   **Barbless**

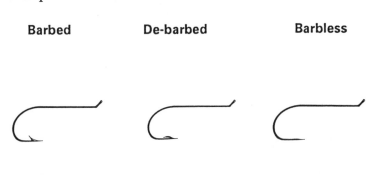

Here are some pointers to release a fish unharmed:

• Land the fish as soon as practical—don't "play" the fish until it's too exhausted to survive.

• Release the fish, if possible, without lifting it from the water. A fish out of water is suffocating and in addition is many times heavier. It can pound itself fatally if allowed to flop on the beach or the rocks. Even a few inches of water under a thrashing fish acts as a protective cushion.

- Wet your hand prior to grasping the fish, as a dry hand will more easily remove the fish's protective coating, making it subject to a fungus-like disease.
- Don't touch or grab the fish's gills. These are its"lungs" and are easily damaged.
- If it is difficult to remove the hook from a squirming fish, try holding it upside-down while you extricate the hook.
- Don't squeeze the fish too firmly in the mid-section.
- As you release a tired fish *cradle it upright,* in a slower section of water, until it regains its equilibrium—it will swim away quickly when ready!
- If a hook is embedded deeply and cannot be easily and quickly removed without damage (a forceps or hemostat is a handy tool for this—something worthwhile to hang from your fly vest), then cut the leader as close to the mouth as possible. The water and fish's enzymes will corrode the hook in a few days and the risk of harm is smaller than by tearing it out. You'll probably lose more flies in trees and bushes than by cutting the leader and it's much more satisfying.
- If a fish is somehow hooked in the gills and/or is freely bleeding, and regulations permit, by all means keep it, for a bleeding fish's chances of survival are slim at best.
- If a fish is badly exhausted, *you'll need to revive it* by a form of artificial respiration. To do so, hold the fish with its head facing into a steady flow of water, out of the main current. Watch for its gills opening and closing as you cradle its body upright. If the gills are not working, gently move the fish forward and backward in order to get water (and oxygen) flowing over its gills. This may take a few minutes. Don't release it until it has regained enough strength to swim away *strongly* or it will just go "belly-up" downstream. Release the fish in quiet water close to the area where it was hooked.
- *If* you decide to keep a fish for a meal, dispatch it quickly with a blow to the head with a rock. Don't let it gasp for "air" in a creel. Also, any fish will taste best if gutted and cleaned as quickly as possible after being caught and cooked while fresh.

▲ Last fish of the day

• Lastly, think about carrying a small water-resistant camera. A picture of the fish you caught and released will last a lot longer than the memory of a meal. *Catch your limit—but limit your take!*

Which Fly??

One of the most frequently asked questions of a new fly-fisher is, "What patterns and sizes should I start out with?"

One of the key elements to creating and maintaining enthusiasm for any new sport is success at it—in this case, it's catching fish. Therefore, without further study into an entomology course, the best approach is to rely on those flies that have proven themselves over and over for many generations of fly-fishers. Mentally review what the water is telling you in terms of what is happening (rise forms) and what is most likely to work. These patterns imitate a variety of "bugs" in various stages of their life cycle and are proven fish-getters. By selecting those patterns, from each category, that most closely replicate the "bugs" found in your region of the country and the water you plan to fish, keeping the number of patterns in this basic selection to a minimum (at least in the beginning), you'll remain focused on locating likely lies, your approach and technique, thus avoiding the temptation of endlessly changing flies.

The answer to which flies work best for a particular piece of water can be arrived at by the observation and investigative techniques outlined earlier or by seeking up-to-the-minute information at a fly shop closest to the water in question. You will find yourself with plenty of flies, soon enough, as you shop the local purveyors of fishing supplies for advice on fish activity, hatches, suggestions on which species are available, etc.

...tying on a fly to match the hatch ▼

Fly Patterns

Trout	PATTERN	SIZE RANGE
Drys (upwings)		
Imitates:	Adams	#12–22
-Mayflies	Humpy	# 8–16
-Caddis	Quill Gordon	#12–20
-Midges	Royal Coachman	#10–16
	Lt. Cahill	#10–16
	Irresistible	#10–16
	Spinner	#12–22
	Blue Winged Olive	#12–20
(downwings)		
Imitates:	Henryville Special	#10–14
-Caddis	Elk Hair Caddis	#10–18
-'Hoppers		
Wets/Nymphs		
Imitates:	Soft Hackle	#12–16
-Mayflies	Hare's Ear	#10–16
-Stoneflies	Pleasant Tail	#12–14
-Damsel Flies	Zug Bug	#10–14
-Caddis Larvae	Wooly Worm	# 8–12
	Prince	#12–16
Streamers/Bucktails		
Imitates:	Black Dace	# 6–12
-Minnows	Grey Ghost	# 6–12
-Baitfish	Mickey Finn	# 6–12
	Zonker	# 6–12
	Muddler Minnow	# 8–12
Terrestrials	Joe's Hopper	#10–14
	Letort Cricket	#12–14
	Black Beetle	#12–14
	Ant	# 6–22

Continued

Fly Patterns (continued)

Smallmouth Bass	PATTERN	SIZE RANGE
	Small Poppers	#4–88
	Marabou Muddlers *(black, white)*	#6–10
	Matuka Sculpin *(black, yellow)*	#6–10
	Crayfish Patterns	#4–6
	Black Nose Dace	#6–12
Largemouth Bass	Poppers	#1/0
	Mouse/Frog Patterns	#2–4
	Muddler	#1/0–4/0
	Marabou Leech *(black, white, yellow)*	#4–6
	Silver Shiner	#2–4
Panfish *(Bluegills, Crappie, Sunfish, Perch, etc.)*	Assorted Dry-Flies *(Humpys, Hoppers, etc.)*	#10–12
	Small Poppers	#6–10
	Sponge "Bugs"	#6–10
	Assorted Streamers	#8–12
	Muddler Minnow	#6–12
Steelhead	Brindle Bug	#2–8
	Silver Hilton	#2–8
	Skunk	#2–8
	Comet	#2–8
	Burlap	#2–8
	Fall Favorite	#2–8
Saltwater Flies	Lefty's Deceiver *(assorted colors)*	#2
	Blonde	#3/0–1/0
	M.O.E. Flies	#2–4
	Popping Bugs	#3/0–1/0
	Shrimp Patterns	#2–6

Stream Etiquette

Like any other sport or hobby where you need to share the field with others, a few words of common fishing courtesy are noteworthy.

Fly-fishing by its nature can be a relatively tranquil sport (although not when fish are rising all around you and you can't seem to hook-up fast enough or often enough!), so some pointers can help you let others enjoy their sport in the manner that offers minimal disruption and maximum pleasure. For instance:

• If you see another angler fishing a section of good water, don't squeeze in and start fishing the same water just because it is in the public domain. Nothing irritates me more than to be relatively alone on a stretch of stream and have someone come down and fish within 40–50 yards of me, when there is no one else on the river upstream or down as far as the eye can see.

• If you're fishing upstream (or down) and come across another angler as you progress, walk around him with enough room not to disturb his fishing or his experience.

• The temptation is great, after seeing a successful angler, to want to cross-examine him about the type, size, and pattern of his fly, technique, etc. *(Hey...what are you using???)* A little friendly conversation is fine...a rapid flurry of demanding questions is rude...use your best judgment.

• On more and more rivers these days, drift boats are becoming commonplace. The adversarial relationship between shore and boat fishers is unnecessary and counterproductive. Don't cast into the other person's space. They will drift by soon enough.

• Blend in. Just as you should meld with the surrounding as you stalk your quarry, blend in with the environment. Loud conversation and noisy loading and unloading of equipment can be heard for considerable distances in the thin mountain air, disturbing the experience for others within earshot.

• Don't trespass! If it says, keep out—then *keep out*. If you feel the area is that inviting and you think you can approach the owners, then, without assumption (and fly rod) ask permission to either cross or to fish the property. You might gain access to some "private water" that receives very little pressure. If you are allowed entry, close all gates, don't let the live-stock get loose on your account. Also, a thank you in person or by note, after the fact, can give you both the feeling of having done the right thing.

• Litter…a sad thing anyplace, much more so in the pristine setting of a mountain or remote lake setting…one simple word—*don't*. You might even pick up a piece or two.

• Be friendly—you're on common ground with other anglers, both literally and figuratively…a nod, a wave or other friendly gesture and subsequent conversation can offer an opportunity to share a tip or particularly good fly pattern.

The Lucky Seven "Rules"
(to stack the deck in your favor and create your own "luck")

#1. Never fish over vacant water.

#2. Don't scare the fish.

#3. Fish the method and technique most appropriate to the water and conditions.

#4. Make your presentation imitate the natural's.

#5. After picking the fishiest water, get yourself in position to make the most of each cast.

#6. Systematically and thoroughly fish the water.

#7. A fish released today is around to fight another day! (A picture is worth a dozen meals.)

*O*ne final word to the wise regarding the opening day of the fishing season. If you've picked up this book prior to the fishing season, have learned to cast and accumulated your gear, etc., then you're probably chomping at the bit to get to the water.

Opening day can be either great or sometimes a major disappointment to the uninitiated. In many parts of the country opening day is too early for any decent fly-fishing, or fishing in general for that matter. The water is usually unstable, and running high, fast and off-color. There are also more people out on the water that weekend than any other. So, if you're going to go anyway, then go with the right mental attitude and think of it as a dress rehearsal for the upcoming season. Take a friend and seek out some water that's a little off the beaten path. You can leave behind 90% of the other fishermen by walking up or downstream a half-mile or so from a stream or lake's initial access point.

North Clark Fork, Alaska—Two brothers take a break from fishing below the glacial source of the river. ▼

Prepare ahead by making your calls to check on the areas with the best conditions. Check your map and plan your route a few days before you plan to leave. Buy your license before you leave home. Rural stores may not be convenient to your waterside destination or they can even run-out of forms on opening weekend. If you're unfamiliar with the area's fishing restrictions, check the regulations regarding hooks (barbed *vs.* barbless), size and bag limits. The more prepared you are, the better time you'll have.

Most of all — ***Have Fun!!!***

Rainbow Trout —

Dark olive to bluish green back to silvery body with uniform black spots on body, head and tail. May be silvery in lakes and reservoirs. Pink "rainbow" coloring along the lateral line.

RAINBOW STRIPE

Brown Trout —

Dark brownish back with dark spots generally on a light colored "halo" background. May have some red or orange spots.

ORANGE AND
RED SPOTS

Brook Trout —

Dark olive, mottled or worm-like lines on back and sides. Light spots on a dark background with some red or pink spots with blue color concentrated on lower half of body.

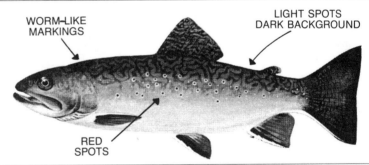

WORM-LIKE
MARKINGS

LIGHT SPOTS
DARK BACKGROUND

RED
SPOTS

Cutthroat Trout —

Black spots on back and concentrating towards the tail over olive/yellow coloring. Distinguished by red or orange "Cutthroat" slash under lower jaw.

DARK SPOTS
LIGHT BACKGROUND

RED SLASH

Golden Trout —

Green/black back, shading down to golden red/orange coloring on flanks, sometimes crossed with olive vertical bars. Black spots concentrated towards the tail.

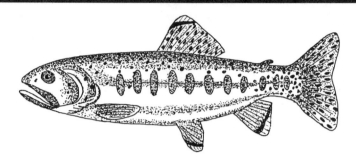

Grayling (trout) —

Olive/green/brown coloring, and distinguished by coarse scales and large dorsal fin.

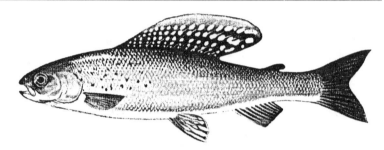

Smallmouth Bass —

Brown or bronze colored back shaded to yellowish-green with variegated vertical dark markings. Shallow notches between spinous and soft portions of dorsal fin. Mouth does not extend quite as far back as the eye.

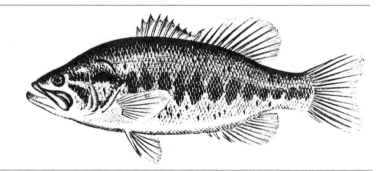

Largemouth Bass —

Blackish back shaded to green. The spinous and soft portions of the dorsal fin are almost separated. The largemouth's upper jaw extends behind the eye in the adult.

Let's Tie One On!

9

I **gave a lot of thought** about whether or not to mention the subject of fly tying in a beginner's book on fly-fishing since there's more than enough to learn regarding selection and refining of your equipment, location of fish, and technique to keep you busy for some time without the added facet of learning how to tie a fly. I include this last chapter on fly tying because not only is it a natural follow-up to fishing with a fly, but it also completes the loop in fooling a fish with an artificial...*one which you've personally tied!*

Fly tiers probably start tying for any number of reasons: an interest in fully exploring the sport, to save on the cost of commercial flies, the ultimate challenge of tying into the big one with one that you tied yourself, a search to create a "killer" fly, or any combination of the above. Whatever the reason, it not only adds a deeper dimension to the sport, but often becomes a hobby unto itself, and a way to stay connected to the sport during the off-season.

It is easy enough to get started on your own with a minimal investment, but it goes beyond the scope of this book to go much further than the very basics. If the information that follows, and a trial fly or two based on it are of interest, there are several good books and excellent instructional video tapes available on the market. There is also a good possibility that fly tying classes are given at your local fly shop that can offer you hands-on instruction.

Although there are a number of "experts" that can tie flies without any equipment other than the materials needed to tie onto the hook, they are the exception. To get started you'll need a fly tiers vise and a few improvisational or store-bought "tools."

The *vise* holds the hook securely in its jaws while the tier wraps the materials on it and *builds* the fly. There are any number of entry models available in the $25–50 price range that are quite satisfactory. As you go up in price, features and options increase proportionally. These include various finishes, height and angle adjustments, rotational heads, separate bases, and mini/macro jaw features, etc.

You'll also need a good, sharp small *scissors* ($4–8) with fine points for cutting and trimming the fly's materials. A *Bodkin* ($1–3) or dubbing needle is extremely helpful for a number of tasks from applying head cement, separating feathers, roughing up and picking out dubbing fur, to cleaning out glue from the eye of the hook. A *bobbin* ($4–6) is extremely convenient for holding the spool of tying thread and for maintaining the proper thread tension to build a strong, well-proportioned fly. *Hackle pliers* ($3–4) make the task of holding the tip of the hackle feathers much easier as they're wound around the hook. A *whip-finisher* ($4–6) enables you to tie-off a neat, durable "knot" quickly and efficiently, to complete the fly.

These are the "basics." Beyond these there are *hair-stackers* to align hair used for wings and tails, *bobbin threaders* to facilitate running the tying thread through the bobbin's tube, *half-hitch* tools to aid in the tying of half-hitch knots, *hackle-gauges* to measure hackle length to the hook size, and all kinds of assorted gadgets to organize and assist you in holding, handling and storing your tools and materials. The basics above, however, or improvisation of same, will get you started.

Next you'll need a few materials, the most obvious of which are some *fly hooks*. There are a number of hook brands to choose from on the market in a range of sizes and styles depending on the type of fly that you wish to tie. O. Mustad & Son, Inc. is one of the oldest and best known brands and probably accounts for the greatest number of fish landed on a fly. Boxes of 100 hooks are the most popular and economical, however you might want to consider a 25-hook package until you settle into the size and style that you prefer to tie. ***Tying thread*** is a necessity, as is some ***head cement*** used to seal-off and cement the head of the fly and the whip-finished knot.

Last, but certainly not least, you'll need to get some *"fur and feathers."* The simplest way to approach this, so that you don't over-buy a bunch of stuff you don't need or won't know what to do with, is to first select a fly pattern or two that you want to try and buy only those few materials necessary to tie that specific fly. This is helpful in a number of ways: by keeping it simple you can keep initial costs down to a minimum and learn to *properly* tie the fly on which you're concentrating—you'll also have less of a tendency to "overload" your first fly by getting too creative, using everything you own and imitating nothing! (I'm speaking from experience).

Since we began our fly-fishing experience with a wet-fly, it's only natural to tie our first fly as a "wet." The water's pressure on this fly pattern flattens the hackle causing it to look like wings and appendages giving an impressionistic image of a number of aquatic insects and its subtle movement also suggests "life." It is, therefore, a good all-around proven fly that will take fish.

Typical fly tying setup. ▼

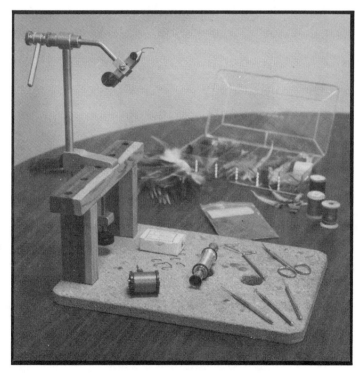

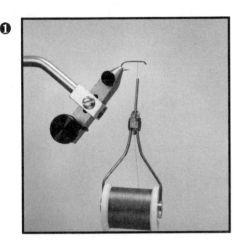

Soft Hackle Fly

Material needs:

Hook: Mustad #3906B or similar
Thread: orange
Body: orange floss plus dark hare's mask dubbing
Hackle: brown partridge/grey guinea

Set up your vise in a well-lighted area, thread the bobbin and line up your tools and materials.

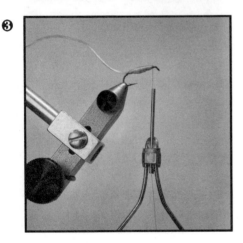

❶ Next, place the hook in the vise just behind the hook's point, as illustrated, and securely lock it into the vise's jaws (but don't overtighten it or you'll weaken the hook). Hold the end of the thread onto the hook's shank, a little behind the eye and wrap it around the shank a couple of times to secure it.

❷ Next, lay the end of the floss just behind the thread and proceed to wrap the thread rearward to secure the floss and provide a level base. Stop at the hook's bend and wrap just the thread forward.

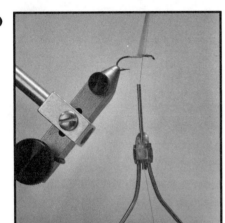

❸ Now, evenly wrap the floss forward over the thread base, stopping at the point of beginning. As you hold the floss in place, wrap the thread over the end of the floss two or three turns to secure it, then cut the floss flush with the thread.

❹ Next, take a *small* amount of the hare dubbing between your thumb and forefinger and twist it into a "noodle" onto the waxed tying thread.

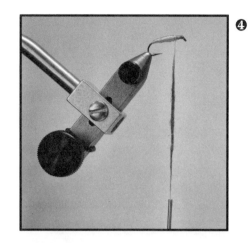

❺ Wrap three or four turns of this furry mixture ahead of the floss and behind the eye to form the fly's *thorax*. Make sure that you leave sufficient room on the hook's shank behind the eye for the hackle and to tie off the whip-finished head.

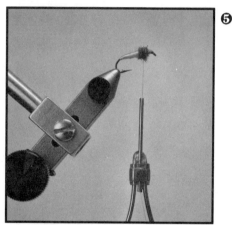

❻ Select a partridge feather and pick or pull out the fuzzy "web" fibers located near the butt-end. Peel the fibers from one side of the feather and tie the butt-end of the hackle's stem to the hook's shank. Make two turns of the hackle by holding its tip with either your fingers or hackle pliers, making the first turn snug against the dubbed thorax, the second in front of the first. Tie off and trim the end.

❼ Now, whip-finish the fly's head (instructions on how to do this will come with the whip-finisher) or tie it off with two or three half-hitch knots.

Last, put a drop of head cement on the head with the tip of the Bodkin to seal and secure the knot. *Your creation is complete!*

This is a quick and easy fly to tie and will teach you the basic elements of fly tying: maintaining good thread tension, sparseness of material, size and proportion. This will become increasingly important as you venture out into more advanced patterns. Patience, good materials, and a few tools are all you'll need to get started and to give you the total satisfaction of completing the connection by successfully fooling, hooking and landing a fish with a fly that you *created with your own hands!*

Resources

Clubs, Associations and Conservation Organizations

You may, like myself, not be much of a "joiner" but an association with one of the following can help you meet, and share ideas and information on technique, equipment and great places to fish with other people with whom you have a common interest. It's also an effective way to concentrate and use the leverage of the club's membership to voice concern and make changes on environmental issues that impact our fisheries. Membership dues, which are nominal, usually include a window decal or embroidered patch to identify yourself as a fly-fisher, a monthly magazine or newsletter outlining the club's activities, special enhancement projects or other newsworthy bits of information on events, tackle shows, new fly patterns, discounted travel, "hot" spots to fish, etc. Check with the national headquarters for the chapter in your area.

Atlantic Salmon Foundation
100 Park Avenue
New York, NY 10017

American Casting Association
7328 Maple Avenue
Cincinnati, Ohio 45321

American Rivers Conservation
317 Pennsylvania Avenue, S.E.
Washington, D.C. 20003

Assoc. of Northwest Steelheaders
6168 N.E. Highway 99, #102
Vancouver, Washington 98665

California Trout
Box 2046
San Francisco, CA 94126

The Federation of Fly Fishers
Box 1088
W. Yellowstone, Montana 59758

Friends of the River
Fort Mason Center, Bldg. C
San Francisco, CA 94123

Oregon Trout
Box 19540
Portland, Oregon 97219

The Nature Conservancy
1800 North Kent Street
Arlington, Virginia 22209

Trout Unlimited
800 Follin Lane, Suite 250
Vienna, Virginia 22180

United Fly Tyers, Inc.
Box 220
Maynard, Mass. 01754

Wildlife Legislative Fund
50 West Broad Street
Columbus, Ohio 43215

Selected Additional Reading

∎ Books: *Strategies/Technique*

Master of the Dry Fly. 1977. Stoeger Sportsman Library.

Masters of the Nymph. 1979. Nick Lyons Books.

Joe Humphreys's Trout Tactics. 1981. Stackpole Books.

Trout Strategies. 1978. Ernest Schwiebert.

Fly-fishing Strategy and Selective Trout. 1975. Swisher & Richards.

Flyfishing. 1982. David Lee.

Reading the Water. 1988. David Hughes, Stackpole Books.

Flyrod Steelhead. 1982. Bill Stinson, Frank Amato Publications.

Float Tubing. 1989. Deke Meyer, Frank Amato Publications.

Flyfishing in Salt Water. 1986. Lefty Kreh, Nick Lyons Books.

Western Fly Fishing Vacations. 1988. Nanci and Kirk Reynolds, Chronicle Books.

∎ Books: *Fly Tying*

Master Fly Tying Guide. 1972. Art Flick, Crown Publishing, New York.

Universal Fly Tying Guide. 1979. Dick Stewart, Stephan Greene Press.

Western Trout Fly Tying Manual. 1974. Jack H. Dennis, Jr., Snake River Books.

∎ Magazines

American Angler	*Fly Rod and Reel*
California Angler	*Outdoor Life*
In-Fisherman	*Sports Afield*
Field and Stream	*Trout*
Fly Fisherman	*Western Outdoors*
Flyfishing	*Backpacker*

Maps

U.S. Geological Survey	**U.S. Geological Survey**
Denver, CO 80225	Reston, VA 22092

GLOSSARY

Anadromous – A type of fish that normally lives in the sea but returns to fresh water rivers and streams to spawn *(i.e., Salmon, Steelhead, Shad, etc.)*.

Arbor – The shaft or spindle in the center of the reel's spool around which the fly line or backing is wound.

Artificial – Refers to the fly used to replicate the natural it was tied to represent.

Attractor – A bright or flashy fly that entices or excites a fish into taking it and doesn't necessarily imitate any particular insect or natural food source.

Backing – Line put on the reel before fastening the fly line, for insurance against having a strong fish run off with all your fly line.

Belly – The section of the fly line between the rod tip and fly that curves outward. This is caused by the influence of wind or varying current speeds on a portion of the line. Also refers to the larger diameter mid-section of a tapered fly line.

Blank – The rod shaft itself regardless of material. Usually referred to as such before the addition of the reel seat, handle, guide, etc.

Catch and Release – The practice of catching and then quickly releasing a fish back into the water, unharmed.

Crustacean – Any number of life forms that live in the water and have a shell, jointed appendages and bodies *(shrimps, crayfish, etc.)*.

Dapping – A technique in which the fly is bounced *(dapped)* on and off the water, simulating a flying insect laying eggs on its surface.

Drag – The pull on the fly caused by tension on its connection to your line/leader that makes it act unnatural. This manifests itself by the fly moving at a rate inconsistent with the current flow and the natural it is imitating. Also refers to the adjustable mechanism of a fly reel that exerts increased tension or braking action on the withdrawal of the line. "Rim-control" reels have an exposed rim so that the reel can be "palmed" by one hand. Thus "palmed" it exerts drag, slowing the fish by the friction of the spool by pressure on the spool's rim.

Dress – To apply a preparation to a fly, fly line or leader in order to enhance its ability to float or sink, as desired.

Dropper – A short strand of line, attached to, or an integral part of a leader, used to attach an additional fly(s).

Dry-fly – A fly tied with materials that are light and/or buoyant enough to float and designed to imitate an insect on or in the water's surface film.

Emerger – Refers to an insect's rise to the surface of the water during its metamorphosis from one stage in its life cycle to the next.

False cast – A preparatory cast where the line is kept in the air prior to allowing it to fall to the water.

Ferrule – The friction joint that strengthens and connects one rod section to the next.

Float tube [A.K.A. BELLY BOAT] – A floating device consisting of an inner-tube housed within a nylon cloth shell, in the center of which the angler sits while fishing.

Floatant – A water-repellant substance, in paste, gelatinized or liquid *(spray)* form, applied to a fly to help it float longer and drier.

Forage fish – Any number of small fish of the lower food chain eaten by larger fish.

Gills – A fish's feathery, blood-rich respiratory organ that extracts oxygen from the water.

Guide – A fine wire eyelet fastened along a rod blank through which the line is strung.

Hackle – The long, slender feather of a bird or fowl used in the formation of a fly.

Hatch – Refers to multiple emergence of insects from the water as they metamorphose from nymphal or pupa stage, prior to flight. Associated with increased fish activity.

Headwater – The small streams that are the source of a river.

Head of the pool – The topmost *(upcurrent)* section of a pool or other slowed portion of running water *(opposite end of the tail-out)*.

Leisenring lift – A nymphing or wet-fly technique in which the angler first predetermines the location and/or lie of a fish, then raises the rod *(drawing the line taut)* in order to quickly bring the fly to the surface, thereby simulating the action of an emerging natural.

Lie – The suspected or known position and location of a fish holding in the water.

Line or **lining** – Allowing your fly line to land or drift *(before your fly)* directly over a fish.

Littoral zone – The region lying along a shallow shore associated with weedbeds and other aquatic plant life.

Mend – Repositioning that portion of the fly line, between its tip and the fly, that is traveling faster *(or slower)* than the rest. The result of not correcting this formation of "belly" formed in the line, is unwanted, unnatural "drag" on the fly and the probable avoidance by the fish.

Metamorphosis – The physical transformation of an insect from one stage of development to the next.

Monofilament – A single, untwisted strand of synthetic material used in making fishing line or leaders.

Nymph – Refers to either an insect in its creeping, crawling, burrowing underwater stage prior to its metamorphosis, or a fly tied to represent same.

Pattern [*as in fly pattern*] – The design and construction of materials assembled on a hook to imitate—in specific, general or impressionistic form—a natural insect or other food form eaten by fish.

Pocket water – A relatively small, quiet section of water protected from the current, found around boulders, downed trees or other obstructions that divert and/or break the water's force.

Pram – A short, square-bowed boat used for fishing.

Presentation – The act of delivering the fly within the target zone suspected to contain fish in a manner that closely imitates the natural that the fly represents.

Prospecting – A generalized searching for fish by using any number of different fly types, patterns or fishing techniques prior to settling on a more specific approach.

Read – The observation and analysis of the various clues *(water temperature, insect activity, types of water, etc.)* that lead you to conclude how, where and when to fish the water to its maximum potential.

Riffle – Slightly broken, rapidly moving water, usually relatively shallow, caused by irregular subsurface rock and rubble.

Rise – The movement of a fish from its station or lie either to take an insect or your fly.

Rise form – The visible tell-tale water disturbance of a fish's activity that offers a clue as to where it is and on what it's feeding.

Roily – Cloudy, unclear, agitated water usually occurring during spring run-off or after a heavy downpour or other disturbance that unsettles the water.

Seine – A fine-woven, small, hand-held net used to strain running water to determine the type and size of insects.

Selective – Refers to fish that have a decided preference for one or another insect in size, color or pattern, usually during a hatch.

Steelhead – A migratory variety of rainbow trout that goes out to sea and returns to its native river to spawn.

Stillwater – Ponds, lakes, reservoirs or other water impoundments or areas in otherwise moving water, where current isn't a factor.

Strike – Refers to either the fish attempting to take a fly or your reaction and response in attempting to set the hook.

Strip – Retrieving or taking in line by pulling it in by-hand as opposed to reeling it in. Also refers to short pulls of the line to give the fly action or "life."

Structure – Subsurface matter *(submerged or downed trees, brush piles, rock rubble, etc.)* that offers fish cover and security.

Tailout – The lower end or bottom section of a pool or run.

Terrestrial – Any insect, bug or small animal normally found living on the land *(crickets, grasshoppers, ants, beetles, mice, etc.)*.

Tippet – The finest end of a leader to which the fly is attached or material tied on to extend its length and usefulness.

Tiptop – The top-most guide that is affixed to the end *(tip)* of the fly rod.

Turn-over – The action *(unrolling of the loop)* of the fly line and leader as the energy of the forward cast propels it forward, to properly lay the fly on the water as intended.

Twitch/tweak – A short quick movement given to a fly to make it show life.

Vacant water – Water known to have "poor" fishing results, for whatever reason. As important, it means reading the water to avoid these areas and fishing *specific* areas of productive water suspected to hold, hide and feed fish.

Wet-fly – One tied with materials and a design that will allow it to quickly sink underwater and imitate any number of different floating, drifting insects or other food forms.

Window – The area of water above a fish where it can see through to the surface with relative clarity.

Wind knot – The unintentional, unwanted formation of a knot in the leader caused by a fault in the execution of the cast.

EPILOGUE

This book, nor any book for that matter, can teach you everything you need to know to successfully fish every technique, for all species, under different conditions. There are literally dozens of good books out there, by writers, past and present, that offer both their personal experiences and instruction on specific techniques, in many cases on individual species of fish. The book is still being written, so to speak, on the *how*, *when* and *where* to fly-fish around the country and around the world. The books listed in the resource section are but the proverbial "tip of the iceberg" in terms of what is available.

As you develop your own individual preferences for either running, still or salt water, the insight, direction and style of other writers offer a wealth of information and can help you refine and perfect the skills necessary to maximize your success. The *challenge* of fly-fishing is what makes and keeps it interesting.

By far the best teacher, however, is experience...your own. No book can adequately describe how to discern the outline of a "seam" that belies a potential feeding area, the subtleness of a trout mouthing your nymph in moving water, or what constitutes "fishy" water. You need to spend time on the water to see and experience these things for yourself. You'll not only develop an appreciation for the conditions that abound, but will also better relate to what you have read, and will want to read in order to further enhance your knowledge of fly-fishing. It's part of the game and part of the fun. ***Enjoy It!***

NOTES